10 REASONS

 TO STAY

Christian

 IN HIGH SCHOOL

A Guide to Staying Sane When Everyone
Else Has Jumped Off the Deep End

MICHAEL ROSS & GREG JOHNSON

goTANDEM.
An Imprint of Barbour Publishing, Inc.

© 2015 by Back to the Bible

Print ISBN 978-1-63058-375-0

eBook Editions:
Adobe Digital Edition (.epub) 978-1-63409-449-8
Kindle and MobiPocket Edition (.prc) 978-1-63409-450-4

The authors are represented by and this book is published in association with the literary agency of WordServe Literary Group, Ltd., www.wordserveliterary.com.

Published by goTandem, an imprint of Barbour Publishing, Inc., P.O. Box 719, Uhrichsville, Ohio 44683, www.barbourbooks.com.

Our mission is to publish and distribute inspirational products offering exceptional value and biblical encouragement to the masses.

Member of the
Evangelical Christian
Publishers Association

Printed in the United States of America.

Stuff in This Book

Know What You Believe
and Why You Believe It

Ever felt that outside of a few well-known stories you don't know too much about the Bible, even though you're pretty sure you're a Christian? Ever been stuck when someone asks, "What does a Christian really believe?" Ever felt that you couldn't let others know the real you—especially the spiritual side of you? And have you ever been frustrated because you were too afraid to reveal to others the person inside, who really does believe what the Bible says, who's convinced that the human race is more than a cosmic accident?

If you have, then you're in a massive amount of great company.

But it doesn't feel so hot, does it? Christians have struggled at times with having family and friends thinking weird thoughts about us. Our beliefs have been laughed at, our motives sometimes mistrusted, and we've felt the agony of defeat when it comes to communicating the most important thing—*the most important Person*—in our lives. It is frustrating and demoralizing. Sometimes it's depressing.

And then if people start accusing you of being bigoted or unloving to those who don't act or believe the way you do, it can get even more discouraging.

What's the answer?

It's not enough to just *know* a few basic facts abour our faith;

we need to *believe* them and *live* them every day. That'a the goal of this book.

We've filled these pages with plenty of Bible wisdom, facts, advice, and tips that will help you do one thing with confidence: show others that you're a real person with real beliefs about a God who is crazy about you—and them. Consider this your guide to staying sane when it feels as if everyone else has jumped off the deep end!

And to help you stand confidently for what you believe, we've identified ten hot-button faith issues along with insights on why Christ-followers hold certain beliefs—or what we call your "ten reasons to stay Christian in high school."

When you start reading these pages, you'll see that we're hitting two main areas where Christians are viewed as not having much to say—in the classroom and in our lives.

IN THE CLASSROOM

We want you to know what to say, as well as how to say it, when your faith is challenged by teachers or classmates. Though it's not important to be a "Bible answer person," there really are answers to tough questions about what we believe. About half of this book will give you the tools you need to help you be understood. We identify situations where Christian students are commonly challenged (and sometimes ridiculed) for their faith, and we paint several real-life scenarios about public school life to give you a good start when it comes to verbally defending—or simply explaining—the real you.

Realize that there's a difference between being understood

and being believed. Helping others *understand* where you're coming from is your responsibility. Getting someone to *believe* is up to God. It's His job to bring others into a relationship with Him; it's our job to represent Him as best we can.

In Your Life

As a Christian, being understood is only half the battle. You see, many outside the church will not be too impressed with your great logic and well-thought-through answers to the tough issues of faith. To quote an old phrase: they want to see a sermon rather than hear one. And the way you live your life will speak louder than any perfectly delivered speech.

The fact is, some Christians are misunderstood because their lives don't come close to matching what they say they believe about God and the Bible. And though the Bible makes it clear that none of us can bat 1.000, people want to see the heart of a believer. They won't be able to relate to a perfect lifestyle, so don't put moral perfection on your checklist. But they will be attracted to a genuine heart. A good heart that cares for others will get them to ask questions. And when they do, wouldn't it be nice to have a few answers? Our dilemma is that many of us treat ourselves or others poorly, we're judgmental, and we honestly don't have a clue about what our lives are actually communicating.

This job of living what we believe is a lifetime assignment. We cut ourselves slack because we know God does. We aren't scared off by lingering doubts because we know God isn't. And we don't give up on people because we know God never will.

What is the next step you need to take toward becoming

more like Jesus Christ? That's what God wants you to ask yourself. It's one rung up the ladder at a time. No leaps and bounds needed or expected.

So join us, and discover your *ten reasons to stay Christian in high school.* . . .

Reason 1

CREATION AND THE CREATED MATTER

I (Mike) was heading through the supermarket checkout lane awhile back when—*pow!*—a headline from one of those crazy tabloids jumped right off the page at me: "Stunning New Scientific Evidence Proves Man Descended from the Flea."

"Say what?" I gasped. "Evidence? Proof? Who *actually* believes this stuff?"

Then a chilling thought shot through my mind. Every day in classrooms across the country, students just like you are having their own "close encounters" of the equally weird kind.

Check out this scenario: Professor Petridish, your first-period science teacher, points to a big chart showing a hairy, apelike creature evolving into a hairless bodybuilder.

"My friends," he announces as he peels a banana and takes a bite, "these are your ancestors. You evolved from the ape. And the way you guys monkey around, I'm not surprised!"

While the room breaks up into laughter, your stomach knots up. *Why is he teaching this stuff as* fact? *Why isn't creationism taken seriously? Should I speak up—or clam up?*

Ultimate Lame Responses

- "Gimme a break, Mr. Know-it-all! Science hasn't proven a thing. In fact, most scientists are so blinded by their own egos and high IQs, they'd like us to think they're the ones responsible for the human race."
- "Wake up, class! Don't you see what's happening? Evolution is yet another trick of the devil. It's an evil

scheme designed to lead God's creation away from the Creator and down a path straight to H-E-L-L!"

- "Okay, I admit it. Some of the stuff in the Bible sounds like major storybook material. I mean, really—the entire earth and everything in it glued together in just six days! I have my doubts. But I have my doubts about what you're teaching, too. So here's the deal. You believe whatever *you* think is right, and I'll do the same. Hey, don't step on my toes with *your* opinions."

- "*Evolution?* No way, dude. The only one in my family who even remotely resembles a monkey is my sister. But trust me, with her moods, she's not of *this* world!"

A BETTER RESPONSE

We're convinced that the biblical perspective on human origins matters. While we love and appreciate animals of all shapes and sizes, it's obvious humans have a qualitative difference to them—a spark, a soul. Could big bang evolution really knit your body together with such perfection? Do you truly understand how complicated the human body, including the brain, heart, muscles, nerves, digestive system, and—most stunningly—the sexual parts, really is?

So, should creationism be presented in the classroom? And if so, by whom?

The law in most states and counties says that teachers can't talk about intelligent design or creation by a God of love who actually knew what He was doing. But you are still allowed freedom of speech and expression anywhere in America. Yes, even in a public school. So every Christian student has a right to respectfully and responsibly share what he or she believes.

Following are some valuable tips—and a pretty good strategy—to help you stand firm even when the pressure makes you squirm. Try this eight-key plan:

Eight Keys to Unlocking the Truth

Key 1: Don't argue, and don't try to act like Mr. Expert.

Your goal should *never* be to blow a classmate or the teacher out of the water, show them up, or *prove* how wacko their arguments are. Your job is to share in a logical manner what you've learned from the Bible and from science, and to allow others to either accept it or reject it.

Since you probably won't change the teacher's mind, a good goal is simply to plant a seed of doubt so your classmates won't swallow the evolution theory without at least questioning it.

Key 2: Get the facts straight.

EVOLUTIONISTS BELIEVE. . .

All life gradually evolved from a single cell, which evolved from dead matter (or perhaps some kind of "big bang"). In the beginning, there was only empty space. Then dust appeared on the scene, followed by gases and chemicals. Where did *they* come from? That's one mystery scientists haven't yet figured out. Eventually everything developed by millions of random changes over aeons of time.

Many (but not all) scientists believe in the big bang theory, which supposedly took place about twenty billion years ago. They say that this material, as a result of gravity, gathered into a huge primordial cloud. After ages it compressed into an immense, unbelievably hot ball, which finally exploded. This explosion flung these same elements into space. More aeons later, gravity caused them to form into millions of smaller balls. And ages after that, they became stars, planets, and galaxies. At some point, these heavenly bodies began rotating in space in an incredibly accurate and predictable manner. All by random chance! This is a pretty fantastic theory, isn't it? But here's the strange deal: most people accept it as truth without examining it. Why? Because that's what many have been taught from kindergarten up. But the truth is, it's only a theory—not scientific fact.

CREATIONISTS BELIEVE. . .

All life and our existence came by the acts of a living, loving Creator. Since their original inception, cells have built themselves from carefully designed and coded information that has been passed from one life to the next.

When creationists use the term *creation*, they are speaking of the original creation of the cosmos—a cosmos in fully working form. Many creationists accept the Bible's historical account, which describes a unique, onetime creation event that took one week and resulted in a complete world, including sea and land, trees, moon, stars, fish, birds, land animals, and man (all fully formed, in that order). Some Christians would say that all this happened in one week; others would say that a "day"—as written in the Bible—could be a thousand years (see 2 Peter 3:8).

Understand that all Christians do not agree on God's method of creation. Did He create the universe in one week, or did He use an evolutionary process to accomplish His goal?

It is beyond the scope of this chapter to attempt to account for *every* theory that Bible-believing Christians hold. Our purpose is to give ideas that will help you—and others—question the "facts" taught in most public schools.

Key 3: Look closely at what evolutionists are arguing.

Despite all the scientific gobbledygook, there are two basic definitions you should know: *microevolution* and *macroevolution*. (It's not really that complicated, so hang with us!)

Scientists studying microevolution can observe small changes within the same types of living organisms. This perspective is valid and actually in line with biblical teaching. In fact, it's not really evolution at all. Dogs will interbreed, and the world will end up with a new breed of dog. But this dog is still a dog.

So what evolutionists refer to as microevolution—change within a created kind—was orchestrated by God to help preserve life. In some ways, it's a survival characteristic. Different species experience *small changes* so that they can adapt to a *changing environment*. But they are not transforming into a different species.

On the other hand, macroevolution suggests that over millions of years a dog could evolve into, say, a horse. And that an ape (or a flea, if you believe the tabloids) could one day become a person.

Evolutionists who hold this view claim that the original clump in the primordial soup became a cell, somehow got life, and then divided. One cell ended up on land and became the ancient ancestor of plant life. The other cell stayed in the water to eventually evolve into boneless sea creatures. After millions of years, one of these creatures—by random chance—became a fish with a backbone. And that, these evolutionists say, is the real beginning of humankind.

Something isn't adding up. Of course, advocates of this viewpoint wouldn't agree. They point to what they claim is their proof: fossil records. Fossils are ancient forms of plant and animal life embedded in sedimentary rock in the crust of the earth, and they are found all over the world. There are "graveyards" that contain the fossilized bones of dinosaurs and other huge animals and birds, as well as those of small animals (including apes and early man).

In 1974 scientists claimed they discovered the long-sought "missing link" between apes and humans. An expedition to Ethiopia led by Donald Johanson, president of the Institute of Human Origins, painstakingly pieced together a remarkable ancient primate skeleton. Although about 60 percent of the skeleton—including much of the skull—was missing, the scientists believed that the apelike primate had some characteristics that were significantly humanlike. They named this "proof" Lucy (or in scientific jargon, *Australopithecus afarensis*).

Key 4: Ask for proof of macroevolutionism.

Know what you'll get? You guessed it: Z-I-P. The truth is, macroevolutionism is a theory with *no evidence*.

Check out the observations of Charles Darwin—one of the world's early advocates of evolutionism and a staunch defender of the "macro" view. In Darwin's own words: "As by this theory innumerable transitional forms must have existed, why do we not find them embedded in countless numbers in the crust of the earth?"[1] In other words, for macroevolution to be true, scientists would have to unearth fossils showing a gradual, step-by-step development of lower animal life into more and more complex forms. No such fossils exist. The millions found are all of highly complex forms of life. The absence of fossil records (of transitional species) proves that it hasn't happened, current observation proves that it is not happening today, and genetic research proves that it could never happen. In other words, a dog just can't evolve into a horse, and an ape can't develop into a man.

Hmmm. . .even Mr. Macroevolution himself couldn't find evidence to support his claims!

Key 5: Point out that macroevolutionism is not scientific fact.

Crack open any basic biology textbook and pinpoint the traditional definition of the *scientific method*: "principles and procedures for the systematic pursuit of knowledge, involving the recognition and formulation of a problem, the collection of data through observation and experimentation, and the formulation and testing of hypotheses."[2] (Translation: If you can't duplicate it in a laboratory, you can't call it scientific.)

Next, locate the definition of a *scientific hypothesis*: an unproved assumption or "an educated guess."[3]

Now point to the fact that since macroevolution cannot be observed or measured (partly because of the lack of a fossil record), it's just a theory and can only be presented as speculation—*not fact*.

Key 6: Show the logic of creationism.

The evidence needed to support creationism is a fossil record that shows complex life appearing suddenly—with no fossils that show lower animals developing into new and complex forms of life.

Guess what? That's exactly what scientists have discovered. They've learned that throughout history, higher categories of living things—fishes, reptiles, primates (including man)—appeared on the scene abruptly.

GOD'S AWESOME CREATION

Think deeply about the origins of life and ask yourself this question: How could this mind-boggling universe, with all of its intricacies, come into being just by chance? Take man, for example. The human body is a marvelously constructed and complex machine. Examine the most visible part of the body: the skin. In magnified pictures, you can see skin layers, blood vessels, oil glands, hair roots, pores, nerves, and pigment.

One-fourth of all the bones in the body are in the hand. With the hand, an artist can do the most delicate painting and a construction worker can lift heavy beams. Each fingerprint is unique.

Study the digestive system and see how everything works together: the pancreas, liver, gallbladder, lymph glands. And think about how the eyes work. Or what about the brain? It's so complicated that even the most complex computer comes no-where near its efficiency. Not only does the brain control the body, but we use it to think and create, to put people in outer space, to feel, to live, and with the spirit, to reach out to God.

So the question is, how could such complex and coordinat-ing systems happen by random chance then evolve over millions of years?

Key 7: Point out the second law of thermodynamics.

This scientific law of physics states that all things run down, not up. Anything left unattended falls apart.

How does this relate to the evolutionism-creationism de-bate? Since living and nonliving things gradually break down and become more disorganized as time passes, it's illogical to believe that matter could have had the capacity to go from a nonliving, disorganized state to a living, organized one.

The fact is, all uphill processes (such as growth) are temporary and require a separate, intelligent force to put them into motion. (Get the picture?)

Key 8: Lastly, drive home your point with a handy word picture—the "airplane comparison."

> *Question:* What part of an airplane flies? Is it the fuselage? The cockpit? The wings? The wheels?
>
> *Answer:* No *single* part can fly. In reality, an airplane is a collection of nonflying parts. The only thing that flies is the total, organized airplane.
>
> *Key point:* These nonflying parts have no capacity to organize themselves into an airplane—*somebody had to do it*.

Now connect your word picture with a living cell.

> *Question:* What part of a cell is alive? The protoplasm? The cell wall? The nucleus?
>
> *Answer:* No *single* part of a cell is alive. A living cell is a collection of nonliving parts. The only thing that makes the cell alive is the total organization of nonliving parts.
>
> *Key point:* These nonliving parts have no capacity to organize themselves into a living cell. Therefore it's logical to say *somebody had to do it*. (That somebody, of course, is God.)
>
> *Conclusion:* The whole issue of the origin of man is primarily a faith issue and can't be proven with observable, scientific facts. But the truth is, creationism

is more in tune with the laws of science than evolutionism is.

This kind of reasoning casts severe doubt on the idea that life could have formed itself. The Christian faith is not a blind faith. It is a reasonable faith that is based on logic. And this point of view should be represented in a classroom.

TERMS TO KNOW

big bang. According to one cosmological theory, the violent cosmic explosion at an infinitesimally small point from which the universe originated billions of years ago.

entropy. A measure of the disorder in a system. Since the law of entropy states that a closed system evolves toward a state of maximum entropy, critics of evolutionary theory point out that the increasing order and complexity involved in evolution would require some kind of outside, intelligent influence.

evolutionary naturalism. The belief that the world can be understood only through the application of evolutionary science and that no account needs to be taken of supernatural or spiritual forces.

fossil record. A record of the fossilized remains of various organisms, arranged in a "geological column" in a manner that—conventional science asserts—broadly reflects the evolution of species. Creationist critics of conventional science claim that the fossil record is inconsistent and not complete enough to warrant this conclusion.

hypothesis. A provisional explanation for a natural

phenomenon. For a hypothesis to have scientific value, it must account for most of the relevant data, and—at least in theory—it must be subject to disproof.

macroevolution. Evolutionary change that involves large and complex steps (such as the transformation of one species into another).

microevolution. Limited genetic changes at the species or subspecies level.

natural selection. According to evolutionary theory, the process by which organisms with traits that better enable them to adapt to environmental factors (such as predators or scarcity of food) will survive and reproduce in greater numbers.

On Your Own

1. Read Genesis 1:1–2:25. Why do you think non-Christian scientists reject this biblical account of creation?

2. Jot down things about the story of creation that are hard to accept. Where does faith fit in?

3. Think about how amazing your body is. Next think about the world, then the universe. Now focus on the Creator. Read Isaiah 40:26 and spend a few minutes jotting down all the mind-boggling things that God created.

4. Read Isaiah 45:18; Romans 1:25; and Ephesians 2:10; then complete the following:
   • What do these verses say about God?
   • What do they communicate about the human race?
   • Name one reason God created people.

5. Read Psalm 148. Make a list of the things you are thankful that God created.

With a Group

1. Has the theory of evolution poked holes in the biblical account of creation? Why or why not?

2. Why does it take just as much faith to buy the evolution theory as it does to believe in creationism? Is evolutionism actually just a religion?

3. How do dinosaurs fit into the picture?

4. If you were asked to give proof of creationism, how would you respond?

5. Give three reasons people say creationism should be taught in public school and three reasons others say it should not be taught in public schools.

Should:

-
-
-

Should not:

-
-
-

Reason 2

FRIENDS ARE WORTH IT

Jason yanks the hamburger out of Brock's hand and takes a bite. "Go on, banana brain. . .ask her," he mumbles while chewing, then opens his mouth and exposes the contents.

"*Gross!* You just nuked my lunch, gorilla breath."

Eric slams his algebra book on Brock's fries—*wham!*—and scrapes the remains into a nearby trash can. "*That's* what I call gross," he says with a grin.

"You're history," Brock snaps. "I'm gonna rip your lungs out through your armpits and knock your—"

The guys freeze as a gaggle of freshman goddesses walk by.

"Babealicious alert," Eric blurts.

Jason falls on his knees and mock stutters, "P–p–p–please, Brocksters, you just g–g–g–gotta help us!"

"Not even," Brock snaps. "With you rejects around, I'm not goin' anywhere near those girls!"

"But they talk to you."

"And with your help, they might even talk to us," Eric adds.

"I'd rather eat maggot intestines."

"You're my best friend," Jason pleads.

"Friends help each other," Eric interjects.

"They don't kill a guy's lunch."

Jason holds up a french fry. "My last one. Take it."

Brock's eyes light up. A grin slowly forms on his lips. He flicks a french fry off Eric's book then high-fives Jason. "Deal!"

Lisa and the Gossip Gang

Lisa's face flushed as Heather filled her in on the latest gossip from Shelly.

"I hate her," Lisa exploded. "I can't believe she's spreading those lies. I hate Shelly so much I could strangle her, and I think I would if I had the chance."

"And I thought you two were best friends," Marsha said.

"Yeah, girl," Heather interjected. "Aren't you, like, twins? We don't see one without the other."

Lisa practically choked on her burger. "Us. . .best friends! Get real. I'd rip her eyes out right now if she came around here."

Rinnngg. . .

The lunch bell sent the girls off to home economics. Lisa swung by her locker to snag her textbook. She fished out a couple of pens and slammed the door shut. *How dare that Shelly?* Lisa thought. *She may be Miss Cheerleader, popular with the senior football players. . .but just who does she think she is?*

Lisa trotted down the hall, shot around the corner, then stopped.

"Hey there, Lisa," Shelly squeaked, throwing her arms around Lisa.

"Oh, uh. . .hi, Shelly." Lisa flashed a grin then brushed her hair out of her eyes. "So, uh, how's my. . .friend doin' today?"

"Couldn't be better." Shelly pressed closer to Lisa. "Hey, have I got some juicy news about Heather. Come by my house after school, okay? Let's invite a few of the girls over. We'll have a great time!"

"Ah, sure. . .after school. . .a few *friends*. . . Wouldn't miss it!"

THIS IS *FRIENDSHIP*?

Hanging out with terrorists at a toxic waste dump would be less hazardous. Sometimes friends treat each other more like enemies than friends.

Leave it to your pals to do dumb things at the worst possible moments.

Guys: Your friends belch right when the best-looking girl at school finally says hi, pull pranks that aren't funny, and spill pop all over your new basketball shoes—then blame it on someone else.

Girls: Your friends blab secrets when they shouldn't, make you feel like crawling into the nearest hole when your new boyfriend comes around, and sometimes make you wonder if being a hermit isn't such a bad option.

But face it: you wouldn't have it any other way, right? You take a few jabs and risk some bruises now and then because friendship is important.

When push comes to shove, most friends stick with you better than the gooiest slice of pepperoni pizza. Your buddies also help you blast the boredom bug—they're good for more laughs (and screams) than the world's fastest triple-looping roller coaster. And whether or not you realize it, they help you grow and learn more about yourself. Sometimes the only way to figure out what you're really thinking or feeling is to talk things out with a friend. And when you're with your friends, you can be yourself; it doesn't matter if you drool or have a big wad of gum stuck in your ear.

But friendships aren't always smooth sailing. The constant "playful" jabs sometimes start to sting and somebody gets hurt. And as with Lisa, there are too many times when our lips flap before our brains kick in.

Here's what's even worse: at times it's hard to pick out the Christian kid from the crowd. Some churchgoing teens hide their faith—playing "secret agent" on campus—and often don't act any different than their non-Christian peers.

What kind of friend are you? And when the pressure is on, how do you react?

MARSHELLA'S MEGASIZED MESS

During lunch Marshella didn't feel like eating with her friends on the lawn—the cool spot to hang out. She slipped into the school cafeteria and tried to blend in with the crowd.

As she unwrapped her cheeseburger, she noticed Megan at a nearby table. *She looks pitiful*, Marshella thought.

Megan sat alone, with her nose in a large textbook. Without batting an eye, she mechanically reached into a sack with her right hand and pulled out food. Marshella noticed how that same hand trembled whenever someone nearby verbally hit her with an insult.

Oh Lord, I guess she's not that bad, Marshella began to pray. *If she would just comb her hair. And those clothes! Why does she wear those Brady Bunch outfits? She's definitely the kind of person Pastor Jeff is always talking about in youth group: "Learn to be an ultimate 'Jesus-style' friend to* everyone*."* Marshella got up and made her way toward Megan's table. *Here I go, God. This is my chance to—*

"Hi, Marshella! Whatcha doin' in here?" her friend Deanna interrupted.

Marshella's body jerked. "Oh, hi. . . Ahh, just eating another gourmet lunch."

Deanna flashed a mocking grin. "Looked like you were about to talk to Megan. I don't understand you. Do you actually like her?"

"Like her? Well. . .ahh. . ." Suddenly Marshella couldn't think straight.

Deanna folded her arms. "Frankly, I'm getting the feeling that your taste in friends has gone to. . .nerds!"

"*No*, Deanna. I *don't* like her, okay?"

"Then help us pull a friendly little prank on Miss Megamess?"

"Prank? What are you up to, Deanna?"

"Derek wants you to invite her to a skating party this weekend. We'll put her on wheels and watch her thrash around the rink. It should be good for a lot of laughs!"

"I don't know, Deanna—"

"Thought you weren't a megageek fan!"

Marshella's heart raced. Deanna's friendship was important to her, but she knew it was wrong to hurt others. *If I do it, I could never live with myself. But if I don't, it's social suicide for sure. Lord, help!*

Ultimate Lame Responses

- "Hey, I'm in. Think I'm a megageek fan?" Then justify to yourself later: *Look, I can't commit social suicide. And anyway, this girl doesn't have friends. . .so it doesn't matter. After all, I'm the one who has the most to lose. My rep is on the line.*

- Agree to pull the prank then apologize to Megan later.
- "Ahh. . .I can't. I just remembered an important family outing that day. My aunt is sick and we have to visit her. Yeah, that's it. But otherwise I'd love to join in on the fun."

A BETTER RESPONSE

Understand the facts of friendship:

A true friend is:	A true friend is not:
someone who accepts you just the way you are (despite a few jabs)	someone who constantly aims his or her word-bullets at you
someone you trust	someone who runs when the going gets rough
someone who sticks up for you	someone who's phony
someone who listens	someone who uses you
someone who really cares	someone who lies
someone who tries to model Jesus	someone who doesn't care about modeling Jesus

FRIENDSHIP FACT: PALS HANG OUT IN HERDS

Name a torture that's worse than eating creamed spinach and more humiliating than one of Aunt Edna's big, wet Christmas kisses. Answer: sitting in a crowded cafeteria—*alone*!

Hands down, this is worse than a dozen wet kisses—maybe even worse than death itself. Enter a room filled with grinning faces you don't recognize (especially if you're the new kid on campus) and your stomach knots up. Your knees shake, your mouth feels like it's full of peanut butter, and that cool new T-shirt suddenly looks like it made a trip through a steam bath.

As you look around the room, you notice something strange (definitely *Twilight Zone* material): everybody is hanging out in herds, or cliques—small, exclusive clumps of guys and girls who share the same interests. Keep looking—you'll see all kinds of herds: jocks, surfers, skaters, science buffs, computer gamers, drama dudes, even *geeks*!

You already know friendship is important. But why does it feel so weird to do a solo step? And just why do guys and girls hang out in herds, anyway?

One word: *acceptance*. No one wants to be left out. When a small group of friends takes you in, you don't have to worry about being alone.

Are herds bad? Well. . .yes and no.

Jesus hung out with a herd: those who followed Him. They often met by themselves for prayer, teaching, and good times. But whenever outsiders came along, the group opened up to them. Jesus was not selective in whom He befriended—He accepted everyone.

If your herd slams the door on strangers and alienates others (makes them feel like aliens), it's time to quit being lame and head for better pasture. Hang out with guys and girls you feel comfortable with, but don't build huge walls around your group. Reach out.

FINDING THE RIGHT HERD

Just about the time the school year kicks into high gear (usually right around midterms), you've probably settled into a pack of pals you'll stay with for the rest of the year. But how can you be sure you'll be able to keep them? How can you be a positive influence on your herd?

"The best way to *have* a good friend is to *be* a good friend." This is a very old proverb, but it's still true today.

If you want to stop clashing and start firming up some solid friendships, remember these important facts:

You're not alone. The people you hang out with have exactly the same pressures and problems as you. Let them know that you respect them and that they're important to you.

Get real! People will see right through you if you're phony. Be the kind of person others can trust by being honest with yourself and with them.

Give a grin. Smiles are important: they enable you to communicate acceptance without saying a word. So, guys, when your friend is having an especially bad day, pop a breath mint, pucker up, and smack him in the kisser with a super-slobbery, Aunt Edna–style smooch. (Just kidding, of course.) If that's not your style—or if he's bigger than you—an exploding fist bump will do.

Learn to care. Too often people put themselves before others. But learn to do just the opposite. Reach out to your buddies and put their needs first. Being sensitive to the feelings of others is a skill. Horsing around is one thing, but constantly hurling insults or laughing at people's mistakes can hurt. When a tough time hits, they'll remember who *not* to go to.

Though it seems like kindness doesn't come easily for some teens, you'll be surprised at how many friends you can make—and keep—by being understanding. By covering for others when they mess up and trying not to make them feel foolish, you may end up with a lifelong friendship. Here are some keys:

Turn off your tongue. Be a good listener. Ask a question; then close your mouth and show that you're interested.

Watch those wounding words. If words can be weapons, they also can bring a healing touch. Say something positive to your friend. Be different and make it a habit to toss out compliments instead of put-downs.

WHEN A FRIEND BREAKS FROM THE HERD

Sometimes friends will try anything to be accepted—even by another group.

Face it, guys and girls, you want to be popular. So a few of your peers—or maybe even you—might compromise once, then maybe a second or third time. Before they know it, they slip over the edge—and right into trouble. Some convince themselves, "I gotta look cool. Besides, this may be my last chance to move up and be really happy."

Know a friend who's slipping? One of the hardest parts

about being a friend is helping your friend when he has moved into a group heading for turbulent waters. It's tough, but it's one of the most loving things you can do.

Make sure you affirm your friend and reject his wrong actions. Tell him you care about him and that it hurts to see him doing what he's doing. You can say, "It's your choice. If you want to continue doing these crazy things, go ahead. But I think it's stupid!" Let him know you're willing to be his friend no matter what.

Here are some ways you can steer a pal in the right direction:

- Talk to your parents or youth leader. Get their advice first.
- Pray. Ask Jesus to show you what to do, and ask Him to use you as His tool.
- Go to your friend alone and talk. See if he or she will get back together with the right group.
- Listen to what your friend has to say. If he or she asks for your opinion, be honest and give it.
- Even if your troubled friend calls you names or laughs at you, keep your friendship open. What your mixed-up pal needs most are *real* friends who really care.
- If necessary, ask God to help *you* forgive your friend.

REMEMBER: YOU ARE AN AMBASSADOR OF CHRIST

Therefore, if anyone is in Christ, the new creation has come: The old has gone, the new is here! All this is from God, who reconciled us to himself through Christ and gave us the ministry of reconciliation: that God was reconciling the world to himself in Christ, not counting people's sins against them. And he has committed to us the message of reconciliation. We are therefore Christ's ambassadors, as though God were making his appeal through us. We implore you on Christ's behalf: Be reconciled to God.

2 Corinthians 5:17–20

What kind of example are you? Whether you realize it or not, your actions are being watched by everybody around you. People hear what you say, and they see what you do, where you go, how you dress, and how you handle victory and defeat. You are Christ's example to others.

Check out Brent's story. This Minnesota teen grew up thinking he was nothing but a zero:

"When I was in seventh grade, I detested myself because I was obese," Brent said. "I remember sitting at home one night and taking a wire clothes hanger and beating myself on the thigh until I had big welts. I hated myself.

"But then I met a very special Christian teacher who showed me that God loves me just the way I am. I desperately wanted to see Jesus in the life of somebody. I wanted someone to put their arms around me, and I wanted to know that those were Jesus' arms. I liked the way my teacher represented God. Through him I met God."

Remember: you don't have to be a paid evangelist or a "super Christian" to be a good ambassador. By your life, you can point others to the Truth, the Way, and the Life.

FRIENDSHIPS BEGIN WITH Y-O-U

So just where is Jesus in your friendships? Do you take Him to school with you? Do others see a reflection of Him in your life?

"I saw Him through my teacher's kind words and affirming smile," Brent said. "And despite all the bad stuff I'd heard about myself, I slowly learned that I was okay—because Jesus made me. Even 'fat slob' *me!*"

But life's pressures can be immense. On some days, you wake up and don't feel very Christian. That's when you need to get near the heart of God. And this brings us to another key to great friendships. It can be summed up in one word: growth.

Okay, okay. . .so you may have seen this cute little acronym in youth group. But hey, it works! So hang with us and check out this six-step GROWTH plan to success:

Go. . .and keep your appointments with God.

Do you have a regular quiet time with Jesus? In any relationship, communication is important. Make an effort to spend time alone with God every day. Go to Him daily in prayer. Tell the Lord how much you love Him, and talk about your friends and their needs. Develop a consistent prayer time; a time when you come to Him with your praise, adoration, and thanksgiving. Also go to the Lord with your needs.

Be totally honest with God. He knows what you're thinking and what's going on. Tell God about your struggles, and He'll be there to help you.

Read.

Get into God's Word daily. Study the scriptures, memorize verses, and think about how to apply them. As you do this, a ton of great stuff will get imprinted on your heart. Try reading a verse or chapter each night before you go to bed. It'll give your mind something to work on while you sleep. Make this a daily habit.

Obey.

Make every effort to obey what you've read and to follow God's commandments. Again, you'll never bat 1.000, but like any good father, God doesn't want us doing things that harm our soul. If you look at God's Word as a heart-to-heart talk with the most loving person you know, then your mind will begin to shift the way you view His ideas and commands about living life to the full.

Witness (speak up when asked).

Let your life be an example to others. Seek to honor God in all you do. When the Lord gives you the opportunity, be ready to give a defense for the hope that is in you (1 Peter 3:15).

Trust that God will never leave you.

Nor will He forsake you. He will always be there with you.

Hang out. . .with friends who share your values.

This is another way you can grow in God and avoid unnecessary pressure. If your friends are doing things you know are wrong, make sure they don't drag you down with them. You might even consider not hanging out with them.

On Your Own

1. What qualities make a friend an absolute, without a doubt, 100 percent *true* friend?

2. Read John 15:9–17. Name some qualities about Jesus that make Him the ultimate best friend.

3. Read John 13:1–17. From this passage, how did Jesus influence others during the time when He walked on this earth?

4. Name some ways that you, as a Christian, can have a positive influence on your friends.

5. Read Proverbs 27:10 and Ecclesiastes 4:9–10. Why is it important to have friends and be a friend? Jot down the name of a friend who really needs you in his or her life:

Now make a covenant with God to be a prayer warrior in this person's life.

> *Lord, I am making a commitment to pray for*
> _____ *on a regular basis. I will also*
> *do my best to be a solid Christian example in my*
> *friend's life by putting his or her needs first and by*

helping my friend grow in his or her walk with You.

Your name_____

Date_____

With a Group

1. Name a person you would "lay down your life" for (see John 15:13). Why would you do this?

2. What's the single greatest way you can help a friend?

3. Have someone in the group read Matthew 5:43–48.

4. Why is it hard to love those who don't love you back?

5. Think of someone in your life who has been hard to love. Now share with the group some ways that you can be his or her friend. Name a time when following the herd got you into trouble.

- Did you end up compromising your values?
- What messages about you did your actions send to others?

6. Name some actions or situations that destroy trust in a friendship.

- What are some prime trust builders?

Reason 3

GOD'S WORD IS REAL. . .AND RELEVANT

"So, Mark, what's that book with the gold pages, the one on the bottom of your locker? Something for English?"

"Uh. . .no, Ramon. It's a Bible."

"A Bible? No way! I didn't think anyone read that book except grandmas and TV preachers. What's in it?"

"All kinds of stuff. History, poetry, stories about men and women who lived thousands of years ago."

"Sounds pretty boring. Who makes you bring it to school?"

"No one."

"Then why would you ever want to lug it here? Besides, shouldn't you keep it at home? After all, this is a public school, and there is such a thing as separation of church and state. . .not that I really care."

"Actually, there's nothing illegal about bringing a Bible to school, Ramon. Just because it's a public school doesn't mean I can't read what I want to in my spare time. Have you ever read any of it?"

"Me? No way. I'm not religious. Looks like you are though."

"I'm not really religious. I'm a Christian. There's a big difference. Want to hear about it sometime?"

"Sorry, Mark, I'm not into it. Here comes Kathy. Ask her; maybe she is. Hey, Kathy. Ol' Mark here has a Bible, and he's trying to tell me he's not religious. You ever hear of that?"

Ugghh! Not Kathy. Now she'll never talk to me. Lord, is this the price of bringing my Bible to school? What if word gets around? Everyone's going to think I'm "religious."

ULTIMATE LAME RESPONSES

- "Um. . .hi, Kathy. Ramon was just being an A-number-one jerk here, trying to tell me I couldn't bring my Bible to school. Have you ever known someone so ignorant?"
- "I gotta get to class."
- "Listen, Ramon. The Bible is God's Word. You know what that means, bucko? It means that ignorant sots like you are going to fuel the fires of hell unless you start reading it. And even though you're gorgeous, Kathy, the Bible doesn't say that your good looks are going to get you to heaven. You both better listen to me while there's still time, or you'll be pickin' hot embers out of your hair for a few million years."
- "Hi, Kathy. Ramon's giving me a hard time for bringing my Bible *one* time to school. That doesn't make me religious. Besides, I brought it to show my English teacher [*lying*]. Hey, you going to the game this Friday?"

SOCIAL SUICIDE?

Unfortunately, the last thing most teens want is to be a dead giveaway. Especially when it comes to the religious label, which sometimes blackballs Christians from a social life with the cool crowd. After all, what would you think about some Muslim who brought the Qur'an to school and started carrying it around? You'd probably think he or she was a religious weirdo, right?

Most people who have no Christian background think the Bible is a boring old book with too many words and not enough pictures. On the surface, they're right. It doesn't exactly resemble Call of Duty, Facebook, or *Sports Illustrated*.

Defending the Bible against skeptics may be the toughest dilemma—yet the most important issue—a Christian high schooler has to navigate. Friends will give you weird looks or ask tough questions you really don't know how to answer. Some of their questions will even be pretty good ones (that is, you may not have the answers right at your fingertips):

- Wasn't the Bible written too long ago to be relevant today?
- Why do so many parts seem not to make any sense?
- Are you sure it's historically accurate?
- Aren't there some errors in the Bible?

While we can give sound reasons for believing that the Bible is God's Word (which is one goal of this chapter), don't expect your average pre-Christian to buy into this conviction. Here's why:

1. Movies and television don't exactly put the Bible or Christians on a high pedestal. Most of the time, Christians are the brunt of jokes or made to look like crazed religious fanatics.

2. If your classmates are not Christians, you can sometimes conclude that their parents aren't either. That may mean these students have already heard a bunch of negative stuff about the church and about pastors, priests, and Christians in general.

3. Perhaps your friends have had a bad experience with "religion." Since Christians are human—and do make mistakes—there's a good chance your friends have seen or heard something that turned them off.

There's not much you can do if these three things are clouding their ability to look at the Bible without biases, but you can be ready to talk about why you hold the Bible in high regard, if they ask.

REASONS GOD GAVE US THE BIBLE

A guy once told me (Greg) to try to convince him about Christianity without using the Bible. He truly believed there was nothing of value in it. The reason? It couldn't answer *every one* of his questions about *every* subject.

What were God's intentions when He gave us His Word?

To show us His true character. By choosing to send His only Son to die on a cross for our sins, God exemplified true, unselfish love. The central theme of the entire Bible—Old Testament and New Testament—is this: God used the Jewish people to bring forth the Messiah, who would save *all* people who would believe in Him.

To give us an "owner's manual" for getting the most out of life. To place us on earth and allow us to make up the rules as we go would have been cruel beyond belief. God's guidelines for how we are to treat each other and how we can get to know Him better are perfectly clear. The Bible is 100 percent accurate in everything God felt was important for us to know. While there is room for debate on irrelevant issues (like whether Judas hanged himself or whether he stabbed himself—see "Resolving 'Contradictions' in the Bible" at the end of the book), there are no discrepancies in His promises, commands, and warnings—the most important stuff we need to know.

To transform our lives. I (Mike) am convinced that connecting with the Bible daily changes the things about us we'd rather leave in the trash can. It actually helps us work through our struggles, resist temptation. . .and live a more peaceful, harmonious life. How's that possible? Well, for starters, consider this about the Bible: "There's nothing like the written Word of God for showing you the way to salvation through faith in Christ Jesus. Every part of Scripture is God-breathed and useful one way or another—showing us truth, exposing our rebellion, correcting our mistakes, training us to live God's way. Through the Word we are put together and shaped up for the tasks God has for us" (2 Timothy 3:16–17 MSG).

Supernatural, transformational, life-changing—yep, there is no other literary work quite like this book. Think about the way in which it was put together: through divine inspiration. Bible scholar Dr. Norman Geisler points out that this fact alone is amazing: "First, there is the source of inspiration: God; second, the means of inspiration: men of God; third, the nature of inspiration: words from God: and finally, the result of this inspiration: the divine truth of God. No other book has been composed in this fashion."[1]

To help us grow in grace. But in order for this to happen, we have to do more than casually read scripture. We need to feed on it, digest it. Here's how Eugene Peterson, author of *The Message*, explains Bible engagement: "Reading is an immense gift, but only if the words are assimilated, taken into the soul—eaten, chewed, gnawed, received in unhurried delight. Words of men and women long dead, or separated by miles and/or years, come off the page and enter our lives freshly and precisely, conveying truth and beauty and goodness, words that God's Spirit has used and uses to breathe life into our souls."[2]

THINGS THE BIBLE WASN'T DESIGNED TO ANSWER

Science. Should the Bible be the final word on subjects like these: What really happened to dinosaurs? How does nuclear fission occur? How many solar systems are there? Why does the sun set in the west? How do you cure heart disease? Why do girls go to the bathroom in groups?

While these are important questions to some, God decided they didn't contribute to His overall plan to reveal Himself to humans, so He left them out. Like a father giving his final message to his wife and kids before he goes off to war, God gave us the things we needed to know *the most* through the Bible.

History. Do we need a year-by-year, detailed, 100 percent infallible description of history in order to believe God created us for a reason? Again, that would be great for us to have, but it wouldn't change the central theme.

How accurate is Bible history? If you skim through the Old Testament, you can see that it mentions many matters of a historical nature: kings, rulers, peoples, nations, confederacies, military campaigns, political customs, and great battles. It would be ridiculous to assume that every solitary historical reference in the Bible has had confirmation from an outside, impartial source. But archaeologists and researchers are constantly making new discoveries that confirm Bible history.

Geography. If God wanted to prove His existence, why didn't

He make the Bible say things like "The world is round"; "The Garden of Eden can be found in. . ."; "Noah's ark is really on Mount. . ."; and "The world's tallest mountain is Mount Everest"?

Do you need to know this stuff to realize that God loves you enough to send His only Son to die on a cross and pay the penalty for your sin? We hope not.

Whenever people have had access to good data on science, history, and geography from other sources that were in turn authoritative, we have never been able to find any scriptural discrepancies that stand the test of time. When the Bible does speak on these subjects, it is authoritative. Actually, trying to cross-reference what we know compared to what God knows is like authenticating time from the Greenwich observatory (where the world's official time is kept) by checking it against a $2.69 digital watch bought at a gas station. He knows infinitely more than us. In truth, it's arrogant for humans to believe that God should have to prove Himself to us by supplying us with specific details on every topic.

THE BIBLE IS UNIQUE

- It features sixty-six books by forty authors (from every walk of life, including kings, peasants, philosophers, fishermen, poets, statesmen, scholars), yet it is totally consistent.
- It has had a tremendous influence on people.
- It was written over a period of sixteen hundred years on three continents (Asia, Africa, Europe).
- Parts of it have been preserved for over four thousand years.

- It answers people's deepest questions—about purpose, death, eternity.
- It is archaeologically accurate.
- In the Old Testament, there are 318 prophecies about the Messiah that were all fulfilled by Jesus.
- The modern translations of the New Testament are
- extremely accurate and reliable. By way of comparison, in every one of Shakespeare's thirty-seven plays (in existence just over two hundred years), there are approximately one hundred readings still in dispute, many of which materially affect the meaning of the messages in which they occur.

How Was the New Testament Put Together?

Back in the 1800s, ancient Greek texts of the New Testament were divided by scholars into "families." The scholars had noticed that some manuscripts had similar characteristics, based on what part of the world they were discovered in.

The major families of texts are Alexandrian (Egypt), Byzantine (Turkey), Caesarean (Israel), and Western (Roman). The families given the most weight in terms of authority are those that are shorter, more difficult, and more ancient (mainly the Alexandrian texts). The Byzantine texts are in more abun-dance, but they are longer readings (meaning that scribes added words as they copied), and they are not as old.

But even between these four families, there is no discrepancy in the meaning of the texts. Any discrepancy that does exist is just a matter of a few peripheral words.

How Can You Be Sure the New Testament Really Is Accurate and Reliable?

There are more than 5,330 Greek New Testament parchment fragments still in existence, some dating within a century of the apostles. Also, we have some eight thousand Latin parchments and hundreds more in dozens of other ancient versions. (It should be noted that there are still this many intact despite the fact that the Roman emperor Diocletian had a standing order that all scriptures be burned if discovered. Many Christians chose to die rather than "deny the faith" by surrendering New Testament scriptures for destruction.)

As further corroboration to New Testament accuracy, within two hundred years all but eleven verses of the New Testament were quoted by early church fathers, in 36,289 citations.

Are all of the passages in these scraps of parchment the same, word for word? Actually, no. But that isn't a cause for alarm. If *you* copied a book of the Bible then checked it with your original, you'd find a few misspellings and some *a*'s turned into *the*'s. Does this mean that the text's message is different or that you messed up an essential doctrine of the faith? Not likely.

Scholars *are* certain of the *exact* wording of all but four hundred words in the New Testament. Nearly all of these are tense issues, minor word changes, and a few added words that assist in clarity for that particular language.

Let's look at the writings of some men in early history—men about whose existence historians have absolutely no doubt—and compare them to the New Testament:

Person	Lived (Wrote)	Earliest Copy	Number of Copies of Writings in Existence
Caesar (*The Gallic Wars*)	100–44 BC	AD 900	10
Homer (*The Odyssey, The Illiad*)	900 BC	AD 1400	643
Sophocles (Greek dramatist)	496–406 BC	AD 950	193
Euripides (Greek dramatic poet)	480–406 BC	AD 1180	9
Plato (Greek philosopher)	427–347 BC	AD 940	7
Aristotle (Greek philosopher)	384–322 BC	AD 1100	5
Demosthenes (Greek orator)	384–322 BC	AD 860	200
Lucretius (Roman poet and philosopher)	96–55 BC	AD 930	2
Livy (Roman historian)	59 BC–AD 17	AD 500	20
New Testament	AD 40–100	AD 130	14,000

Check the encyclopedia in your school library for these names. Most likely it will cast no doubt on the fact that all of these men existed. Talk to your history teacher. He or she will likely recognize and affirm that history proves that these men existed and that the literature ascribed to them is reliable. Yet try to talk about the authority of the Bible based on the overwhelming amount of recent copies of original manuscripts, and he or she will likely find some way of explaining it away. Some adults simply believe what they choose to believe, even when the evidence points in the opposite direction of their "facts."

Your teenage friends at school, however, are a different story. They are not set in their ways and beliefs and are much more open to the truth of God's Word. True, they may need some questions answered, but if some of the logic and facts in this chapter are explained, they may indeed give the Bible a second look. By helping to establish its authority, you've broken down a barrier that prevents pre-Christians from allowing God to speak directly to them. Remember, it's not your job to *convince* anyone of anything. Your job is to be ready to defend the faith as best you can.

WHEN AND WHY WAS THE NEW TESTAMENT PUT TOGETHER IN THE FORM WE HAVE NOW?

In about AD 140, a heretic named Marcion developed his own Bible and began to preach from it. The church needed to offset his influence by determining what the real canon (measuring rod) of New Testament scripture was. Also, many Eastern Orthodox church services were using books that were definitely not from authoritative sources.

It was decided that only manuscripts that could, without a doubt, be traced to those who lived when Christ lived (Peter, Paul, Matthew, John, James, Jude) or to those who had a close association with the apostles would be allowed to be called scripture. (Luke is said to have written Luke and Acts under Paul's influence, and Mark wrote the book of Mark by copying down what Peter said.)

Athanasius of Alexandria (AD 367) gives us the earliest list of New Testament books that corresponds exactly to the books that make up our present New Testament.

HOW DID WE GET THE OLD TESTAMENT BIBLE?

Originally it was passed down orally through men whose job it was to memorize what had been told to them by preceding generations, men whose entire purpose in life was to make sure that succeeding generations knew what God had done among their people. After language began to be written down using an alphabet (about the fifth century BC), the scriptures were copied over and over by scribes. Because the climate caused the material onto which they copied the scriptures–thin parchment (animal skins) and papyrus—to deteriorate over time, copying was a constant process.

Up until 285 BC the Old Testament scriptures were all copied down in Hebrew or Aramaic. This period of history was dominated by Greek culture. Demetrius, the librarian for King Ptolemy of Alexandria (where the world's greatest library was located), had every book except a Greek version of (what we call) the Old Testament. Ptolemy enlisted seventy of his most educated scholars who knew Jewish law and could translate Hebrew and Aramaic into Greek. He asked each to translate the Old Testament scriptures, working separately. After seventy-two days, the work was done—*and each translation corresponded exactly to the others*! This became known as the LXX (seventy), or the Septuagint.

Was the Septuagint an accurate copy of the Hebrew writings?

In 1947 thousands of parchments known collectively as the Dead Sea Scrolls were discovered in Israel. These fragments of the Old Testament have a date of about 125 BC. Among the texts was nearly an entire copy of the book of Isaiah. Before this was discovered, the earliest existing copy of the book of Isaiah came from a scroll called the Masoretic (Hebrew) text. It is dated at AD 916—over one thousand years later. They are nearly the same, word for word! This shows the unusual accuracy of scripture copying over a thousand-year period.

HOW DO ARCHAEOLOGICAL DISCOVERIES HELP PROVE THE BIBLE?

Josh McDowell says that "while archaeology can verify history and shed light on various passages of the Bible, it is beyond the realm of archaeology to prove the Bible is the Word of God."[3]

Archaeology without historical record, however, is pointless. Digging up other people's trash and ruins only tells us of cultural customs and events. It doesn't give us the exact chronology of history (like the Bible does).

"What archaeology has done," says Josh, "is to verify some of the history contained in the Bible. For instance, two of the cities mentioned in the Bible, Sodom and Gomorrah, have been for many years considered mythological by the intellectual community. However, recent excavations at Tell Mardikh, now known to be the site of Ebla, uncovered about 15,000 tablets. Some of these have been translated, and mention is made of Sodom and Gomorrah."

Isn't the Bible Full of Errors?

You'll likely hear this one a lot in your lifetime. It is usually said by those who have never read the Bible and are simply looking for an excuse to stay in control of their own lives. But let's assume it's an honest question coming from a seeking heart. What does the Bible say about itself? Well, there are two passages you can refer to:

All scripture is God-breathed and is useful for teaching, rebuking, correcting and training in righteousness, so that the servant of God may be thoroughly equipped for every good work.
2 Timothy 3:16–17

Above all, you must understand that no prophecy of Scripture came about by the prophet's own interpretation of things. For prophecy never had its origin in the human will, but prophets, though human, spoke from God as they were carried along by the Holy Spirit.
2 Peter 1:20–21

The word "God-breathed" is a translation of the Greek word *theopneustos*, meaning "inspired." Thus the origin of scripture is God, not man; it is inspired.

For two hundred years, there has been a huge discussion among Christians as to whether these passages are saying that the Bible is "inerrant" (without errors) or simply "inspired." The first two words would make you believe that there are no contradictions in the Bible. In fact, there are several passages that *do* seem to be contradictory (see "Resolving 'Contradictions' in the Bible" at the end of this book). We tend to agree with Dr. Ronald Youngblood when he says, "I believe that the original writers' work was inerrant. Those copying it, however, were subject to the kinds of human errors even the most thorough and dedicated scribes can make."[4]

Do the so-called "contradictions" change the overall message of the Bible? Hardly. In fact, any reasonable person would have to admit they do not detract from even the smallest messages of the Bible, let alone the major themes.

IS A MOVEMENT CALLED THE "EMERGING CHURCH" REJECTING THE BIBLE?

Gone are the days when a majority of Christ-followers could share Bible basics—such as naming at least one of the Ten Commandments or identifying at least one of the apostles. Gone are the days when they could articulate how *most* Christian churches view scripture: "a message that's inspired by the Holy Spirit," "divine revelation," "trusted, timeless, and relevant instruction for all believers," "*the* voice of authority."

In reality, the face of Christianity is being changed by believers who are disillusioned with the traditional, "institutional" church and those who advocate a "deconstruction of modern Christian worship and community"—for example, individuals who identify with the emerging church. Who are these people? They're part of more than 58 million Americans who make up two generational segments of our society: yours and your older siblings' generation—mosaics (those born between 1984 and 2002)—and middle-aged folks such as your parents and your teachers—busters (those born between 1965 and 1983).

Mosaic and buster Christians are among those who are often the most skeptical of present-day Christianity.[5] In fact, many don't view the Bible as the authoritative words of the Almighty. They see scripture, and the Christian tradition as a whole, from a different perspective: historical, metaphorical, and sacramental.[6]

WHY IS IT DIFFICULT TO "PROVE" CHRISTIANITY TO YOUR FRIENDS BY USING THE BIBLE?

When Paul used the Old Testament scriptures to persuade people about Jesus, he was talking to Jews who were already convinced of the scriptures' authority. From Paul's example, is it possible to reasonably conclude that a friend at school should also have a high degree of respect for the Bible? If you quote it while making a case for a certain subject, should you automatically assume they should believe your argument just because it comes from the Bible?

The answer to both questions is no. Those outside the church will not have the same respect for the Bible that Christians do.

That leaves you with a choice: you can arrogantly proceed to quote passages that "prove" you to be right, or you can meet these people where they are and reasonably (and often slowly) move them toward checking out the Bible for themselves.

We vote for the latter. Instead of using the truth of the Bible as a club, Christians should hold it high and encourage seeking unbelievers to check things out for themselves. As that happens, the power of God's Word can hit with full effect. When a heart and mind go one-on-one with the Holy Spirit through His Word, God *always* wins!

On Your Own

1. What does Jesus say about the Old Testament? Look up these passages and write down the significance of His words:
> Matthew 5:17
> Matthew 21:42
> Matthew 26:54–56
> Luke 24:25–27
> John 5:39; 17:17

2. What importance does Jesus give to the Old Testament scriptures?
> Matthew 19:4–5
> Mark 12:18–27

3. What do these passages say about the authority of Jesus?
> Matthew 28:18
> Mark 1:27
> Mark 2:10–11

4. When the leaders of the early church talked to Jews and God-fearing Gentiles, how did they try to convince them?

     Acts 17:2–4

     Acts 17:11–12

     Acts 18:28

5. When Paul talked to those who knew nothing about the Old Testament, how did he do it?

     Acts 17:16–34

     Acts 24:10–23

With a Group

Look up the passages and discuss the questions in the "On Your Own" section.

1. What do people at school think or say about the Bible?

2. What is it about the Bible that makes you sometimes doubt that it is actually God's Word?

3. What is it about the Bible that makes you realize that it really is God's Word?

4. What points would you use if someone asked you to prove whether the Bible is *the* authority? Name your top three.

Why Some Believers Don't Read the Bible

A survey conducted by Back to the Bible uncovered more than eleven thousand reasons why Christ-followers don't read God's Word. Here are the top two: *"I'm too busy"* and *"I just don't have enough time in the day!"** But how can this be? Consider this: During a typical workday, the average adult American spends. . .

- 1 hour eating and drinking
- 8.8 hours working (which includes e-mailing, surfing the web, texting, and talking on the phone)
- 1.3 hours caring for others, including children
- 1 hour doing household activities (including cooking and cleaning)
- 1.7 hours doing "other" activities such as surfing the web, texting, and talking on the phone for personal reasons
- 2.6 hours in leisure activities (including watching TV)
- 7.6 hours sleeping†

*Quotes adapted from survey research conducted
by Dr. Pam Ovwigho, Back to the Bible, 2012.
†US Bureau of Labor Statistics, Web Report (bls.gov),
February 23, 2010.

Reason 4

POPULARITY ISN'T WORTH THE CHASE

Is it wrong to be involved with outside activities or excel in school or have a close relationship to help make you feel you're worth something?

Not always, but it can be.

The next time you're walking through the hallways, look around. What you'll see are classmates involved in dozens of activities (drama, sports, band, student government) or types of groups (science club, stoners, thrashers, Christians).

How would these people feel about themselves if their group or activity was somehow taken away from them? Some would be devastated. All they have in life is what they *do* or what group they belong to.

What about you?

What if your abilities didn't measure up or all of your social groups suddenly left you in the dust? How would *you* feel?

Do you have anything inside that would tell you that you're still worthwhile, that you're not just one of five and a half billion people groping their way through life but a unique and special person who was created—for a reason—by a powerful, loving God?

Both Mike and I have known hundreds of Christian students who went to church but still pursued activities and friends that provided the *immediate*—though artificial—rewards they thought they needed.

In a sense, they're Christian-lite, because they haven't grasped just *who* they actually are.

ULTIMATE LAME RESPONSES

- When you start to feel like you don't fit in with the cool people at school, find out where the next Friday night party is and make an appearance. (Extra lame points: get drunk and make a fool of yourself so everyone will be talking about you Monday morning.)
- Realizing that smart people usually don't fit in with the cool crowd, quit studying for tests and don't work as hard in class. That way your grades will get worse and you can have cooler (though slightly less intelligent) friends.
- When a friend at school suddenly gets a bad reputation (like the label "nerd"), act like a nerd yourself by (1) avoiding him or her like the plague and (2) picking on him or her—right along with the crowd.
- Find only one group to hang with, and *never* associate with any other.

Christians have living inside of them the Creator of the universe; but in this area, they've left Him standing just barely inside the door of their hearts. Sadly, instead of allowing God to speak words of truth to them about how special, important, and unique they are, they pursue short-term feelings of self-worth by chasing popularity.

WHAT MAKES PEOPLE WORTHWHILE?

Ask someone you know that question and you'll get answers like this:

> a sense of humor
> trustworthiness

good looks
money
honesty
muscles
a good personality
a trim bod
athletic skills
a high IQ
a supportive family
a cool car

Some of this list makes sense, doesn't it? After all, you wouldn't want to spend time with someone who had a bad personality or who was dishonest. The things on this list may determine if someone is worthwhile to *you*, but does that mean that if people don't possess these things, they're not worthwhile? From the way some people are treated—and the way some people feel about themselves—you'd think so.

But it doesn't!

The reason?

> *But God demonstrates his own love for us in this:*
> *While we were still sinners, Christ died for us.*
> ROMANS 5:8

If Jesus Christ died for all sinners (everyone), this means that each person has value to God. Not just the rich, the good-looking, the intelligent, the athletic, the popular—*everyone*!

The obvious problem is that those who don't know Christ

don't believe it. Do you know why? Because most *Christians* at your school don't believe it either. It's easy to tell—they're simply acting like everyone else who doesn't know his or her own worth, and doing whatever it takes to be popular.

IT'S NOT ALL THEIR FAULT

Let's back off here for a moment. We don't want to be too hard on *every* Christian teen. Some honestly can't help the way they behave or how they feel about themselves. Here are a few of the main reasons:

Their family. If a girl grows up in a home in which her mother worried more about her daughter's *outward* appearance than about her *inward* character, that's likely what the girl will worry about most during her teen years.

If a guy is raised by a father trying to relive his adolescence through his son by pushing him toward sports from a very early age, the son is going to feel good about himself only if he's a good athlete who makes the team in every sport he plays.

If a girl is raised by critical parents who rarely encourage her—even if she only gets one B and the rest As on her report card—she's going to feel like she has to perform at the top levels of academic excellence before her parents will show her love.

If a boy's dad works a lot or is gone from the home, the boy will rarely have the chance to see what a Christian man is supposed to act like. Consequently, he's going to make it up as he goes—and he's not always going to make the right decisions.

All of these situations happen in "good Christian homes." The result is that children don't realize they are loved unconditionally by God. Therefore they act accordingly, pursuing popularity or doing things that make them feel better about themselves.

The crowd. If you're not "playing the game" during your junior high and high school years, you're probably not popular. "Playing the game" is doing those things that are socially acceptable. Though the rules are different at each school—and in each part of the country—here are a few of the most familiar:

- dating popular classmates (or for girls, dating older guys)
- wearing the right clothes
- driving the right truck or car
- going to the right parties
- using the right "language" (swearing)
- having a loud stereo in your car
- not being friends with "nerds"

It's sad but true. Social survival at some schools is dependent on how you measure up in these areas. And if you don't measure up, you're not cool. And if you're not cool, what are you? You're a wannabe. You're trying to break into the cool crowd. And what happens if you can't break in? You feel bad about yourself. You feel like an outcast. You feel like you'll never have any "friends." (And believe it or not, some teens even resort to extreme behavior because they can't break in!)

There *are* those who don't play this game: students who don't care what anyone thinks. Sometimes they're Christians; sometimes they're not.

If there is one goal that Christian students should have during their teenage years, it's to feel secure in who God made them to be. Unfortunately, many are concerned with what the crowd thinks—and are spending every waking moment trying to figure out how to get in with the popular kids.

Most teens don't realize it, but the moment they graduate from high school, all of these people who were so important for so many years are suddenly gone! If you've spent your high school years "playing the game" to fit in, you'll likely keep doing it when you get to college. It's a sad way to live, but Christian teens are choosing this way in every school in America.

The popular culture. Millions of teens think that if they don't measure up to Hollywood's standards—either by looks, personality, or abilities—then they just can't compete. We'll deal more with this later, but it's obvious that TV, movies, and music groups are being used by the father of lies (Satan) to make teens not believe they are really worth something. Females are especially susceptible to comparing themselves to what girls' magazines tell them is the perfect girl.

What do people do when they don't like themselves because of what their family, their friends, or the popular culture has taught them?

Sadly, instead of finding out the truth—how much God values them just as they are—they do four things:

1. They attempt to *numb* themselves from the rejection they feel through alcohol, drugs, pornography, or overeating.

2. They try to *escape* the feelings of worthlessness through astrology, the occult, romance novels, movies, TV, or sometimes suicide.

3. They *mask* their feelings of inadequacy through intellectu-

alism, being the class clown, putting themselves down so others will pay attention to them, or being an overachiever in school in order to please teachers and parents (since they can't please their peers).

4. They *ignore* the rejection and try to please everyone; they put up a good front and in vain continue their attempts to get what they think they need: the approval of the crowd.

How can you listen and believe the quiet truth of what God thinks about you when so many people are screaming in your ear lies straight from the pit of hell?

First of all, you have to want the truth more than the lies. A lot of Christian teens know exactly who they are in Christ, but they refuse to act accordingly because popularity is a more immediate and tangible goal. Jesus said, "Then you will know the truth, and the truth will set you free" (John 8:32). Well, they know the truth, but they haven't allowed it to set them free.

If your self-image is founded on misinformation, your behavior and actions will be inaccurate.

> Definition of self-image: *The accumulation of all the attitudes we have perceived about ourselves since birth.*

> Definition of self-esteem: *The corresponding feeling we have about this image of ourselves.*

God is not a yeller. Though He is constantly pursuing you, He prefers to do it in a quiet, subtle way. Satan, on the other hand, is a raving lunatic. He'll try anything to divert your attention away from the truth.

Second, if you're tired of the game and ready to allow God

to speak words of truth to you, it's time to do something "unnatural." Sit down in the quietness of your room (no stereo, please), and let the invisible God speak the truth to you through His Word. The Bible isn't just for old people, parents, or pastors; it's for *you*! The only way you can *believe* the truth and *act on* the truth is to *know* the truth.

WHAT DOES GOD REALLY THINK OF YOU?

You've heard that God loves you. And you know that God allowed His Son, Jesus Christ, to die on a cross—and pay the penalty of your sin—to demonstrate the extent of that love. Then why don't more Christians act like this is the most amazing news we've ever heard? If God—the One who created us—says we are worthy of *His* love, why do we pursue what our culture thinks we should in order to feel good about ourselves?

We're immature, that's why!

We think the world revolves around us. And it takes a few years of really knowing the true God to realize that *He* is the center of the universe, not us.

Did you notice the emphasis on "true God"? Because of a weird upbringing or a bad church experience, many teens don't really know the true God. They may have different perceptions of who God is:

- He's a stern judge who's only interested in giving commandments to people to keep them in line.
- He's like a heavenly Santa Claus, someone we turn to only when we want something.
- He's still a baby in a manger, not really strong enough to do anything.

The faster your eyes can focus on the *true* God through a

relationship with Jesus Christ, the faster you'll not only believe but feel like you really have worth—just for being who He has created you to be.

The inability to relate to the right God and see yourself from His perspective isn't just a teenage disease either. Adults often carry the same feelings of self-centeredness throughout their lives.

Let's make a quick distinction here: self-centeredness does not always equal selfishness. People can be caring and giving but still not feel worthwhile. Though they've learned how to be nice, they aren't viewing themselves the way God does.

So how can you begin seeing yourself the way God does?

- Read the Word and let the truth set you free from the pressure to please the crowd.
- Memorize a few passages that particularly stand out to you. (A number of passages in the "On Your Own" or "With a Group" sections would be a good start.)
- Hang with friends who tell you the truth—encouragers.
- Practice spotting lies when they come your way. If a teacher, parent, or friend calls you ignorant, recognize that that's not God's opinion.

How do you build others up?

- Tell them the truth about who they are. Be one of the few who remind their friends of their strengths and abilities.
- Making a few friendly put-downs often becomes a habit. Cut back on the cuts!
- Be a defender of your friends when they're in front of you or when someone is talking behind their backs.

- Point others to the One who will always tell them the truth.

Here's a good quote to remember: Treat people as they are, and they will remain that way. Treat them the way God would treat them, and you'll help them become what they were meant to be.

On Your Own

1. Read Psalm 139. Write down what the writer says about the way God looks at us.

2. Look up 2 Corinthians 10:12. What does comparing yourself to others tell about you?

3. According to these passages, how should we feel about our imperfections?
> Isaiah 45:9
> Romans 9:20
> 2 Corinthians 12:9

4. According to these passages, what shouldn't we be worrying about?
> Matthew 6:27–30
> Luke 12:15
> Philippians 4:4–9

5. According to these passages, what is God most concerned with?
> 1 Samuel 16:7
> Micah 6:8
> Matthew 23:23

With a Group

1. Do you like to give your opinion? Now's your chance. Circle whether you (A) agree or (D) disagree with the statements below:

A   D   Everyone has a need to be accepted by somebody.

A   D   To be really happy, a person must be liked by everyone.

A   D   People must prove they are worth being accepted before they can be.

A   D   Many people don't accept themselves.

A   D   Some people will do anything to be accepted.

A   D   Most things people do to try to earn acceptance backfire.

A   D   It's wrong to try to earn the acceptance of others.

A   D   Try as they might, some people can't find anyone to accept them.

A   D   To feel good about yourself, you need to be accepted by others.

A   D   It's important to realize that you are accepted by God.

    Discuss each point and try not to be afraid to share what you believe.

2. Do you tend to concentrate more on your strengths or your weaknesses? How about when you think of others: strengths or weaknesses?

3. According to these passages, what have you been given if you're a Christian?

    1 Corinthians 2:16

    Ephesians 1:3

    Philippians 4:19

    Colossians 1:22

    1 John 4:13

4. According to these passages, who are you if you have Christ?

    John 1:12

    1 Corinthians 3:16

    1 Corinthians 12:27

    2 Corinthians 5:17

    Ephesians 2:19

5. Why has God created you?

    Romans 12:1–2

    1 Corinthians 12:14–27

    Ephesians 2:8–10

    1 Peter 2:9–10

Reason 5

YOUR WORK ALWAYS MATTERS

Do you remember playing the "What if" game when you were a kid? Here are three "What if" situations for you to finish:

THE MISSING MONEY

After a few weeks of being trained by the manager, you were trusted to be on your own as a cashier at a fast-food place. One day your till turned up ten dollars short at the end of your shift. The rule was that your pay was reduced by whatever shortage your register had (when the cash in your register was compared to the amount of sales you rang up).

You told your manager that you were certain you hadn't made any mistakes. Then you remembered a phone call that you had wanted to make about halfway through your shift. Another employee (who had been known for making mistakes in giving change) had been left alone out front where both registers were.

Here are possible steps you could take to make things right. Write down a number next to each step to indicate what you would try first, second, and so on. Cross out those things you wouldn't do:

___ Tell the manager that in two months you've never made a mistake, that you didn't give anyone too much change, that you're honest and didn't take the money, and that it's just not fair that you should be penalized for something you didn't do.

___ Ask the other employee if she used your register. If so, ask whether she made any mistakes on it.

___ Talk to your parents later and ask them to call the manager to try to convince her of how responsible you are and that it was probably another employee who made the mistake and then blamed it on you.

___ The next time you work with that employee, take ten dollars out of her register while she's not around. That will make things even.

___ Even though you know that it wasn't your fault, take responsibility for the missing ten dollars, learn from it (lock your register next time), and forget about it.

___ Have the manager confront the other employee to see if she can intimidate her into admitting what happened.

___ Quit.

___ Ask never to work with that employee again.

___ Admit that you could have made a mistake and take the deduction without arguing or complaining.

___ Other:

Walmart Scam

During the Christmas rush, you land a temporary four-to-nine job at Walmart helping to keep the stockroom in order. The regular employees seem to be nice, and you make friends right away with a few guys your age. Since this is only your second real job, you not only want to perform well, you want to fit in with everyone else. Most of the guys you work with are older and out of high school. A couple of them take you under their wing and show you the ropes.

Your third Thursday night on the job, after your shift, Larry and Troy motion you over to where they're finishing up a task. As you walk over, Troy says he'll watch around the corner and walks past you.

"Hey, Pete, do you have an iPod?" Larry asks.

"No, but I asked for one for Christmas. I'm not going to hold my breath though. My parents are broke."

"Well, you don't have to wait for Christmas. Here, grab one of these and stuff it in your pants."

"You want me to take a brand-new iPod?"

"Hey, you're not stealing it. This whole box is going to be shipped back to the big Walmart warehouse. It's full of stuff that was returned for one reason or another. Walmart sends it back to the distributor and will get new stuff in return. We heard that when a box gets returned, they don't even check what's in it. They just look at what's on the list and ship new stuff to Walmart. The box probably gets tossed or something. So you see, it's not stealing. Just consider it a Christmas bonus from Walmart for a job well done. Do you know how many *billions* of dollars they made last year? I don't think they're going to care what happens to a few iPods that cost five dollars to make in Japan."

"If they don't care, then why should I stuff it in my pants?"

"Look, I'm just trying to do you a favor. Do you want it or not?"

"Well. . ."

Here are possible things you could say and do. Write down a number next to each to indicate what you would try first, second, and so on. Cross out those things you wouldn't do.

___ Take the iPod, but return it later when the guys aren't around.

___ Tell Larry, "Thanks but no thanks. I don't really listen to that much music anyway."

___ Look Larry in the eye. Tell him that what he's doing is wrong and threaten to inform the supervisor about what's going on.

___ Say, "No, thanks," then walk away. The next day, tell the supervisor about what's going on.

___ Figure that God is trying to bless and reward you for all of your hard work; take the iPod and say thanks to Larry.

___ Ask Larry if you can have a day to think about it. The next day at school, talk to a couple of your Christian friends and ask their advice. After school tell your mom about a "hypothetical situation" and get her opinion.

___ Other:

BREAK ROOM CONFRONTATION

You've been bagging groceries at a local grocery store for about a month. You work the six-to-ten shift three nights a week, and then you work all day on Saturdays. The store manager has asked you to work Sundays, but you've told him you'd rather not because you go to church and want to spend time with your family. He hasn't forced you to work Sundays yet, though you can tell he hasn't been too happy about being turned down. He's even said, "The way to move up at this store is to agree to any hours the manager gives you."

One Saturday afternoon, about two o'clock, you're taking your thirty-minute lunch in the break room. Because it's a slow time of day, there are about eight people in there. The conversation moves to what everyone is going to do on Sunday. Heather, one of the older women, mentions that after church she and her family are going out to the lake for a picnic. Two of the younger checkout women laugh and agree they won't be in *any* shape to be getting up before noon tomorrow morning.

One of the managers says that he wouldn't be caught dead in church, that it's too full of hypocrites. He goes on to tell a story of a pastor he once knew who divorced his wife and ran off with his secretary.

That starts the flow of complaints about church. One of the young checkout women says she used to go but they always talked too much about hell. "I thought church was a place where people were supposed to love each other. All I ever felt there was judgment."

A bagger friend you work with says he can't believe people actually would want to follow an old, hard-to-read book and some dead Jewish guy.

Another mentions that church plays an important role in society. "If we didn't have churches, where would people get married? And where would we have funerals? Besides, some people need a crutch to lean on because they're not emotionally strong enough to make it alone. It provides them with friends who are like them."

MICHAEL ROSS & GREG JOHNSON

Heather finally speaks up. "I just think you've all had bad experiences. Church isn't like that at all. Forty years ago I heard that Jesus Christ loved me enough to die for my sins so I could go to heaven. Since I knew I wasn't perfect—and I wanted to go to heaven—I accepted Him into my life. Church helps me learn more about God. It provides a place where I can help others. Helping others—that's what church is all about."

"Help others. . .right!" the store manager says. "Is that why my dad's church, which he went to for twenty years, helped me out of $150 to have his funeral there?" Suddenly he looks at you. "Hey, you go to church every week. Why would a young guy like you want to go? Or do your parents force you?"

"Umm. . ."

Again, here are some possible things you could say or do. Write down numbers next to each to indicate what you would try first, second, and so on. Cross out those things you wouldn't do.

___ "Yeah, my parents have to make me go. But sometimes I like it."

___ "We've been going my whole life. I've never really thought about not going. It's just something our family does."

___ "Whoa, look at the time. I'd better get back to work."

___ "I agree with Heather. Church is somewhere I go to learn more about God. Even though I'm only a teenager, I can still see that life is too tough to try to make it as the Lone Ranger. I really need church."

___ Instead of saying anything about what you believe, repeat what everyone else has said. As you walk out, say, "Everyone's entitled to his or her own opinion."

___ "Not everything about church is wonderful. There are hypocrites who attend. I suppose that's because Christians aren't perfect—they're human. So far, I haven't had too many bad experiences with it, and sometimes I even enjoy it."

___ Other:

WHY SPEAK UP?

All three of these stories are examples of real-life dilemmas you'll face once you join the workforce. The first was a *Christian character dilemma.* Will you, with the right attitude, take responsibility for something, or will you do anything to prove you were right?

The second was a *moral dilemma.* When confronted with the opportunity to do something you know is wrong—and regardless of whether you'll get caught or not—what will you do or say?

The third is a *courage dilemma.* Do you have the strength to stick up for Jesus Christ in the face of opposition, or will you deflate when the pressure hits?

How do you know what the right thing to say and do is without looking like a wishy-washy Christian geek? All three examples illustrate this one truth: *knowing* the right thing and *doing* it isn't easy!

The reason these three dilemmas are essential to ponder isn't to draw attention to yourself and how good you are. It's to present a case for anyone you come in contact with to consider having the God of the universe take up residence in his or her life. The truth: life is really hard, and people are going to need a close relationship with the true God of the Bible in order to make it through.

It's likely true that if we knew there wouldn't be any social (or sometimes economic) consequences for our attempts to represent the Christian faith, most of us would know the right actions to take or words to speak. Ah, but sometimes there *are* consequences, aren't there? So we keep silent or say something that betrays what we know to be true. In the process, we feel guilty or stupid. What's the answer?

Well, that depends. How badly do you want to do the right thing; how much do you care about the long-term happiness and well-being of those you come in contact with? If you're satisfied with being a chameleon (you remember, that little animal that changes skin color to blend in with its surroundings), probably no amount of coaching or convincing will give you the courage to do something you don't want to do.

But let's assume you *want* to be more prepared. If that's the case, here are a few ideas for how to keep firm when your knees are weak.

Rehearse. With a parent, friend, or youth leader, go through as many situations as you can think of that could cause you to do the thing that would represent your true heart the worst. If you know what to expect and what to say—*before* it happens—you'll be much more confident.

But in your hearts revere Christ as Lord. Always be prepared to give an answer to everyone who asks you to give the reason for the hope that you have. But do this with gentleness and respect, keeping a clear conscience, so that those who speak maliciously against your good behavior in Christ may be ashamed of their slander.

1 PETER 3:15–16

Get the word out. Unfortunately, many Christians want to be full-time in God's Secret Service. That is, they want the benefits of being a Christian, but they don't want anyone else to know they are one. You don't have to hand out tracts to inform your coworkers of your allegiance to Christ, but you can drop signals—low-key or high-octane, whatever you're comfortable with—to let them know where you stand. Here are a few examples of things to do or say:

- "Does your family have any Christmas (or Easter) traditions? We go to church on Christmas Eve and. . ."
- Read a pocket Bible or a Christian book on your break.
- "I've got to tell you about this Christian camp I went to last summer. You won't believe some of the things we did."
- Pray before inhaling your lunch.
- When someone mentions a struggle they're going through, let them know you'll pray for them. How? A short note or quick word is often all it takes.

*I am not ashamed of the gospel, because it is the
power of God that brings salvation to everyone
who believes: first to the Jew, then to the Gentile.*
ROMANS 1:16

Let your actions speak loudly. At work your job comes first.
If you're not a good employee, you may end up giving all
Christians a bad name. You're not a slave, but this verse applies
nonetheless:

*Slaves, obey your earthly masters in everything; and do it,
not only when their eye is on you and to curry their favor,
but with sincerity of heart and reverence for the Lord.*
COLOSSIANS 3:22

Don't bad-mouth your bosses behind their backs. It's true that
nearly every employee rags on his or her boss occasionally. So
be unique and don't join in. That alone will show people there's
something different about you.

*Remind the people to be subject to rulers and authorities, to be
obedient, to be ready to do whatever is good, to slander no one, to be
peaceable and considerate, and always be gentle toward everyone.*
TITUS 3:1–2

Hold your tongue. When other workers start telling off-col-
or jokes or making crude remarks, fight the urge to participate.
Don't act superior or judgmental (after all, non-Christians *will*

act like non-Christians); just try to keep quiet or turn away. Yes, this may mean that it will take longer to be included in the "group," but in the long run, what type of reputation do you want: a sheep who'll blend in with the gang because it's the safe thing to do or a person of character who has a firm moral foundation?

Do not let any unwholesome talk come out of your mouths, but only what is helpful for building others up according to their needs, that it may benefit those who listen. . . . Nor should there be obscenity, foolish talk or coarse joking, which are out of place, but rather thanksgiving.
EPHESIANS 4:29; 5:4

TOUGH QUESTIONS
What's more important, the job or my faith?

When you are employed, the big-picture issue isn't how to earn a few bucks to help your parents with your car insurance; it's how to be God's man or woman in a particular place at a particular time. He has strategically placed you in a job not just to pad your bank account but to represent Him to lost souls who (a) may *never* have been prayed for in their entire lives, and therefore need you to fight for them on your knees, and (b) need you to move them up one more notch toward a faith in Christ. It's not your responsibility to save them (it's God's), but rather to be faithful and consistent in your beliefs as best you can, and to be ready to answer—or find the answers to—their questions.

All this is from God, who reconciled us to himself through Christ and gave us the ministry of reconciliation. . . . And he has committed to us the message of reconciliation. We are therefore Christ's ambassadors, as though God were making his appeal through us.

2 CORINTHIANS 5:18–20

What if my boss asks me to do something that I know is wrong?

While this question seems like a no-brainer, Christians will often obey their bosses instead of their consciences. Whether it's filling out your time card differently to prevent your boss from having to do more paperwork, or cutting corners to give the appearance that the job is complete, or telling a white lie to your boss's boss so that your boss doesn't get into trouble—the temptation to fudge on the truth needs to be fought off. Again, it may mean you'll have to take some grief for not "going along," but you must keep the big picture in mind.

People are watching. And though you may not score any points with your boss, coworkers may need to observe strong convictions in action before they decide they want such convictions for themselves (even a coworker not warm to Christianity). That which could help bring another to faith in Christ just may be you getting fired or demoted because you did what was right. You decide. Which is more important?

But even if you should suffer for what is right, you are blessed. . . . It is better, if it is God's will, to suffer for doing good than for doing evil.

1 PETER 3:14, 17

What should I do if my boss chews me out in front of everyone?

Sadly, some bosses abuse the authority they've been given. They feel it necessary to put employees "in their place" in front of others in order to set an example of what could happen to the other employees if they mess up. It's a poor way to manage and actually does more harm than good. A boss needs to have the respect of his or her workers in order for them to function efficiently. Tirades rarely cause workers to respect their boss.

The key issue here isn't whether you deserve the tongue lashing or not; it's your response to the episode. If you can respond patiently and respectfully (even with someone who doesn't deserve it), others will notice. And if they notice, they just might wonder where your inner strength comes from.

If you did mess up, take the medicine that is handed out. Apologize if your boss lets you, explain your side if your boss asks you to, but accept responsibility for your actions. Don't blame it on anyone else.

If you didn't mess up, yet you're getting chewed on anyway—again, take it. Defend yourself in a respectful way if you have the chance, both in front of your coworkers and in private. But when it's all over, fight the urge to get back at or bad-mouth your boss later. Nobody wins when that happens, and you might lose the credibility you've been building up with your coworkers.

When they hurled their insults at him, [Jesus] did
not retaliate; when he suffered, he made no threats.
Instead, he entrusted himself to him who judges justly.
1 PETER 2:23

What if I see a health hazard that's being ignored?

Always report it. If your immediate boss won't listen, call or write a note (anonymously, if you must) to his or her boss with information about what's happening. Keeping silent is never your best option.

On Your Own

1. Look up these passages and apply them to your situation. What are you *really* responsible to do?

> Romans 10:1
> Romans 15:18
> 1 Corinthians 3:6–11
> 1 Corinthians 5:9–11
> Ephesians 5:15–16
> Colossians 1:28–29

2. What do these passages tell you about what Paul's ultimate goal was? How would he benefit by pursuing that goal?

> 1 Corinthians 9:16–23
> 1 Corinthians 10:32–33
> 2 Corinthians 6:3

3. According to these passages, what are we really fighting against?

> 2 Corinthians 4:4
> Ephesians 4:18
> Ephesians 6:11–12

4. How do these passages relate to being a Christian in the marketplace?

> Ephesians 6:7
> Philippians 2:3–4
> Colossians 4:5–6

5. How should you respond if coworkers say you're just a kid?

> 1 Timothy 4:12–16
> 2 Timothy 4:2–5

With a Group

1. What other situations arise in which a Christian is tempted to compromise his or her faith or give in to pressure from coworkers?

2. How does God use our bad circumstances to help others? (See 2 Corinthians 1:3–7.)

3. Can you think of any examples of how God has used your bad times to help others?

4. What will be the consequences for those who live their entire lives separated from God? (See 2 Thessalonians 1:8–10; Hebrews 9:27; 2 Peter 3:9.)

5. What should you do when you are tempted to give up?

> Galatians 6:9
> Hebrews 12:3
> Revelation 2:10

Reason 6

RELATIONSHIPS HAVE A PURPOSE

A Few Pretty Important Things You Need
to Know about Guy-Girl Connections

DUSTIN, IN THE LOCKER ROOM

"She's an absolute ten!" Matt says as he pulls off his practice jersey. He flings it into his locker then pelts Dustin with a sweaty sock. "And she's going with a dweeb like *you*!"

"Unreal," Chris chimes in. "If I dated her. . .ooohhh, dude." He falls to the floor, clutching his chest—faking a massive coronary.

Jesse gives Dustin a fist bump and grins. "So. . .you've been going out with her for three weeks, huh? Just what happens when you two are alone—*totally alone*?"

Dustin shrugs. "You know. . .stuff. We talk. Watch TV. . ."

"*And. . .* ," Jesse presses.

"Eat, study, talk some more—"

The guys bomb Dustin—*plop, thud, smack!*—with crusted gym clothes. Then Matt launches the ultimate question. "Fess up, dude. Has she let you have it yet?"

Dustin looks up and swallows, sirens blazing in his head: *Geek alert—coolness about to be clobbered!*

"Ahh. . .have what?" he asks nonchalantly, knowing full well which "it" his friend is referring to.

"*It*, you idiot!" Matt barks. "Whaddaya think?"

Of course Dustin has never done it, and he isn't going to— until marriage. In his eyes, to move too fast too soon spells major headaches: pregnancy, sexual diseases, broken hearts. And as a Christian, he has even better reasons to wait.

But the guys. . . How on earth can he explain this to them?

Dustin looks Matt in the eye. "And I suppose you have!"

Matt bristles. "Hey, think I'm gay?" he fires back. " 'Course I've done it. . .lots of times. What *normal* guy hasn't?"

Dustin's stomach knots up. He hates locker room talk—especially when his reputation is on the line. He doesn't want to lie, *but*. . .

"Well. . .ahh. . ." Dustin pauses. "Actually, I. . .I mean *we*. . .umm. . ." (Inside, his geek alert suddenly reaches mega-critical status.)

What do I tell them? he wonders as he frantically searches for the precise words. *How do I stand for what's right without being laughed at. . .and without looking like a total geek?*

JAMIE, HOME ALONE

"Brad Purcell!" Amber's voice screams through the phone. "You are absolutely the luckiest girl alive, Jamie Richards."

"It's too cool to believe," Jamie giggles, flopping down on her bed. "It's like an incredible dream, and I don't ever want to wake up. He actually asked me!"

"Amazing! The high school hunk of the century, and he asks *you* to be his girl." Amber sighs.

Jamie presses the receiver to her ear with her shoulder and leans back on her large, stuffed Hello Kitty doll. She begins to draw little hearts on her algebra book cover.

"How does this sound: Jamie and Brad. . .forever!"

"You dork!" Amber laughs. "That's what you said about Sean Mitchell."

"Ooooh. . .don't even mention him," Jamie says. "He was all hands and only had *one* thing on his mind. Brad, well, he's different."

"Earth to Jamie," Amber fires back. "As if I have to remind you, Brad is a guy—a *gorgeous* guy! And *all* guys have only one thing on their minds."

"Whatever, Amber."

"Look, Miss Church Lady," Amber says with that sarcastic tone Jamie hates, "you're not in kindergarten anymore. It's time you grew up a little. Maybe then guys wouldn't dump you so quickly."

Jamie stares at the ceiling in disgust. *Not* this *conversation again. When will Amber get the hint? I'm not that kind of girl.*

"Hey, did you know that my parents went away for the weekend?" Jamie says, hoping to change the subject.

"So you're home *alone?*"

"Yep, the house is mine," Jamie says. "But my parents did leave behind a one-hundred-page list of rules. At the very top is No Guys Allowed!"

"That's perfect!" Amber says.

"Amber, what are you talking about?"

"Jamie, this is your chance. Your parents will never find out."

"Find out what?" Jamie says, deciding to play dumb.

"That you had a secret visitor. And that you and Brad—"

"Forget it, Amber. They'd know," Jamie says. "Believe me, they have their ways. Besides, I just don't. . .I mean, I'd never let a boy—"

"Get down your pants?" Amber interrupts. "*Everyone* is

doing it. So what's up with you?"

Ding donggggg.

The doorbell saves Jamie from Amber's cutting remarks. "Just a sec, Amber. Someone's at the door."

Jamie sets the receiver on her nightstand and darts down the staircase. She grabs the doorknob then takes a quick look out the peephole. She steps back and gasps.

"I can't believe it!" she mumbles to herself. "He's here! He's actually here." She takes another peek. Brad is standing on her doorstep!

She sees Brad shift his weight, glance at his watch, then press the doorbell again.

"Ahh. . .c–c–coming," Jamie says. She spins around and darts halfway up the stairs then stops. *What do I tell Amber? And how do I tell Brad he can't come in?*

Ding dong. Dinggg donggggg. The ringing seems insistent.

Good questions—and it's not just the "cool crowd" asking them anymore.

At one time or another—if you haven't already—you, too, will have a gut-twisting encounter like "Dustin's Dreaded Dilemma" or "Jamie's Gigantic Jam." In the face of sneers, smirks, and rolling eyes, how will *you* respond?

Pop off a steamy *Fifty Shades of Grey*–type romance story and you're cool. But try explaining why you're saving yourself for the honeymoon and—*bam!*—you're suddenly treated like a *major* prude who's missing out on some *major* action. Though some guys and girls have no trouble holding their ground, for others it's worse than facing the dentist's drill.

ULTIMATE LAME RESPONSES

- "Such earthly desires are but a thorn in my side. Yea, though I walk through the Valley of No Sex, I take up my cross and endure. It's hard to be holy, but I know that a crown awaits me in the blessed Promised Land."
- "Sex is wrong! And the minute such earthly urges pounce on my flesh, I take a cold shower. Or I deny them through Bible reading, seven-hour prayer vigils, church attendance. . .and baseball."
- "Have I done *what* before? Hmm. . .er. . .ahh. . .could you repeat the question? I'm just not following you. What is this 'it' you keep referring to? *'It'*? What 'it'? Look, we obviously aren't communicating—so I'll talk to ya later, okay? Bye now."
- "Have I had *sex*? Well. . .er. . .ahh. . .who hasn't? Hey, did ya catch that new show on Netflix?"

A BETTER RESPONSE

The key is to tell the pack that you're not doing it—without being labeled. Impossible? Not if you do these things:

- Stand confidently for what you believe—throughout your life, beginning as early as possible.
- Learn to present the facts and make a few key points that show why waiting is right—even smart.
- Cement the values you've been taught in life, and clear up any doubts swirling around inside your own head.

Whether it's during a heated debate in health class, a scorching confrontation in the locker room, or a game of "phone tag"

MICHAEL ROSS & GREG JOHNSON

with your best friend, try this plan of action:

> *Don't be lame by...*
> - *responding with answers that begin with "The Bible sez..." or "Thou shalt not..."* Not that the Bible is uncool, but as we've said, many teens don't share your belief that the Bible is the ultimate authority. Most will be instantly turned off by rules and "Bible talk." And this kind of response makes God seem like a prosecuting attorney—not a compassionate, forgiving Father. Bottom line: communicate the truth with facts and understandable examples—not with phrases that might sound foreign to others.
> - *stepping on friends who may have blown it (and who just might be feeling a ton of guilt).* Instead, you should present hope and encouragement. Let your pals know that there is a better way.
> - *saying, "I don't know," when you really do.* Nothing will make you (or God) more nauseated than you being lukewarm.

GET A FOOTHOLD ON THE REAL FACTS

Say something like the following:

"I've chosen to wait because I believe that sex outside of marriage can never be safe." Some guys or girls may respond, "If we use protection...then what's the big deal?"

Fact: Condoms are not 100 percent safe and only reduce the risk of contracting a sexually transmitted disease (STD), such as the HIV virus that leads to AIDS. *Reducing* a risk does not mean *eliminating* it.

Most medical doctors agree that in the STD jungle, wearing a condom is safer than not wearing one, but much less safe than avoiding the jungle altogether. The truth is, beyond that thin sheath (which could break) lies disaster—perhaps death.

"I've chosen to wait because I believe that sex is fun, but you can't buy a condom for the heart." Many teens reduce sex to a physical act and to just another way of having fun. To them sex equals recreation. Let others know that you hold sex in high regard and don't want to cheapen this wonderful gift by giving it away to just anyone, that you're saving it for that special person who will be your partner for life.

Fact: Sex is awesome. . .in the right setting (marriage). Unlike anything else a married couple may experience, sexual intercourse creates the deepest, most powerful bond. . .sort of a relational superglue. And that bond is never supposed to be broken. Sex isn't just physical, and it's not a trivial act that feels good for a few seconds and then is over for good. For a couple, sex involves the body, mind, and emotions in an activity that is intended to be shared for a lifetime.

Never buy this age-old line: "Sex will help us really get to know each other." People who say stuff like this don't usually give a rip about the other person or about being intimate. What they really want is sex. And most girls who give in find them-selves alone—until the next guy hears how far she'll go.

"I've chosen to wait because I believe that sex on credit means play now, pay later." You've probably heard one of the following

comments, whether in health class or in the halls:

- "It won't hurt to do it just once."
- "Hey, disease happens to other people."
- "I might catch something? There's probably a vaccine that'll cure it."
- "I might get pregnant? There's a place you can go to take care of it."

Fact: Today's actions will have consequences tomorrow. Don't be fooled into thinking it can't happen to you; you're *not* invincible. Since the period of time it takes to die from AIDS is two to ten years, we'll probably never see *teenagers* succumb from this disease (they'll be in their twenties).

One of the most destructive and permanent results of premarital sex is acquiring an STD. And *anyone* who has sex outside of marriage (even just once) is at risk. Check out these frightening stats from Josh McDowell:[1]

- There are more than twenty different kinds of *incurable* STDs rampant among teens.
- Experts say that of the 1 to 1.5 million HIV-infected Americans, more than one-fifth are teenagers.
- Sixty-three percent of all STD cases occur among persons under age twenty-five.
- In terms of being infected with STDs, if you have sex with someone who is experienced, it's like having sex with all of his or her partners.

"I've chosen to wait because I believe that having sex doesn't make me a man (or a woman)." Ever see a movie or TV show in which the main characters lose their virginity. . .then go through a miraculous transformation: his voice changes or she suddenly looks like a supermodel—and everyone treats them like they're cool? *Yeah, right!*

Fact: You begin to be a *real* man or a *real* woman at the moment of conception. Your gender is firmly a part of who you are and how you were created. Having or not having intercourse has nothing to do with it.

"Not everybody is doing it." But it's little wonder we get the idea everybody is. After all, Hollywood—and even our own government—bombards us with an "everybody does it" message, implying that physical intimacy goes along with dating. Television frequently shows people hopping in and out of bed, and magazines use sex to sell everything from perfume to laundry detergent.

Fact: The mass media is feeding us a lie—and many of our friends are buying into it. But often the steamy stories that guys tell in the locker room are just that—stories. If you're saving sex for the wedding night, you're not alone. Many other teens on your campus have chosen not to be sexually active.

"I'm not weird if I wait." And you won't get sick, go crazy, or die if you don't have sex. Remember, sex is a drive. You need air and food to survive, but you can live a full and happy life without sex. Be assured that all the essential parts work—and you don't need a test run.

Fact: Unlike dogs, cats, and other members of the animal

MICHAEL ROSS & GREG JOHNSON

kingdom that are slaves to their instincts (and that seem to go berserk during mating season), humans are given free choice *and* self-control. God expects us—and helps us—to control our desires and wait for His timing and His best plans for us.

The Lord hasn't given us meaningless guidelines in order to make life boring. And His rules are never dusty or out-of-date. His timeless instructions are intended to protect us from harm and to ensure that we get the most out of the gifts that He provides—such as sex. He's our number one fan and wants us to be happy.

You won't be disappointed if you wait. We guarantee it!

On Your Own

1. Crack open your Bible and check out Leviticus 18:3, 6, 20, 22–24.

- Name some sexual practices that are off-limits to believers.
- From these passages, why do you think God wants Christians to stay pure in such an impure world?

2. Read 1 Corinthians 5:1–13. What will happen to those who don't follow God's guidelines—especially regarding sex?

3. Take a look at Ephesians 5:3 and 1 Thessalonians 4:3–7. Name some sexual standards that God expects of those who wear the label "Christian."

4. Read Romans 7:15. Exactly what is the battle that Paul is talking about?

5. Turn to Zechariah 4:6. This scripture passage reminds us that it is not by our might or by our power but by the Holy Spirit that we are able to withstand temptation. Yes, we'll all fail from time to time. *But when we allow the power of God to help us, we can stand firm.*

6. Write a prayer to God, asking Him to give you strength to stand firm in your faith and power to resist sexual temptation.

With a Group

1. What is God's view on sex?

2. Have different members of your group read the following passages: Leviticus 19:29; Deuteronomy 23:17–18; Proverbs 6:25–29, 32–33. Next tackle these questions:
   - How does God describe prostitution?
   - Why is adultery off-limits for Christians?
   - In what way is sex outside of marriage destructive?

3. Take turns reading portions of Genesis 39 until finished. Now answer these questions:
   - What lessons can we learn from Joseph?
   - In what ways is Joseph a good role model?
   - Will you always be congratulated for taking a stand?

4. Name ten differences between love and lust. (See 1 Corinthians 13:4–7 for some clues.)

5. How far is too far? (Check out 1 Thessalonians 4:3–7 for some ideas.)

Reason 7

LOVE AND RESPECT WIN
WITH THE LGBT ISSUE

Great Responses to Some Questions That Won't Go Away

Here's an actual letter that we received years ago when we were the editors of a magazine called *Breakaway*. As you read it, think about how you'd handle this dilemma.

> *Dear Mike and Greg,*
>
> *I go to a school near a military base. For the past few weeks, we've been discussing discrimination in my English class. One of the projects we had to do was a debate. Our teacher gave us the choice of topics and the chance to be either positive or negative. The topic I chose was "Should homosexuals be allowed in the armed forces?" I took the negative side.*
>
> *In my school, I've been known to stand up for my faith. After the debate, we had to write an argumentative essay on the topic we chose. In mine, I included three things: what most people believe, what soldiers think, and what the Bible says. After handing in the essay I had worked hard on, I was stunned when the teacher gave me a C+. The comment she wrote was shocking. It said I started off well but ended it poorly when I talked about the Bible's law against homosexuals.*
>
> *When I went to complain to the teacher, she explained, "I'm a Christian like you, and I've read in the Bible that masters should be kind to their*

slaves. Today we don't have slaves; therefore the Bible is wrong. That means that homosexuality should be allowed today. If Christ came down, he would probably change the law on homosexuals. Paul was a homosexual and preached that the Bible may be wrong."

I told her that the Bible never said you must or must not own a slave, yet it does say that homosexuality is a sin. She told me that was silly. I couldn't imagine a teacher would say a student's beliefs were silly.

I've already left this event behind, and I'm not trying to get back at her. However, I would like to know what your opinion is and get a better understanding on what the Bible really thinks about homosexuals. In my debate, I expressed that Satan was controlling their lives. Was that a good idea?

Chances are, you've had a similar experience. Perhaps it was a heated conversation with friends at school or at church. . .or an uncomfortable confrontation with a relative who is homosexual. But if your convictions haven't yet been challenged with regard to the LGBT (lesbian, gay, bisexual, transgender) debate, brace yourself, because they will.

So when it feels as if your faith is on the line and you're trapped between a rock and a hard place, what's the best Christian response?

Let's begin with what you should never say. . . .

ULTIMATE LAME RESPONSES

- "All this talk about alternative lifestyles and guys wanting to have sex with guys is making me sick! These are people who have an obvious mental problem. They're in serious need of counseling."

- "My pastor says that homosexuals are an abomination to God. He thinks that God is going to judge our entire nation because we're not only tolerating these people, but our own government is calling evil good and good evil. He thinks that unless we start speaking out against these people, we're all going to pay."

- "To each his own. I really don't have an opinion about homosexuality—and really don't care. I'd rather just mind my own business and let people live the way they want to live. After all, each one of us is responsible for our own choices. Why should I share what I think is *right* or *wrong* behavior? Like I said, to each his own. Live and let live."

A BETTER IDEA

If we're thoughtless with our remarks about the LGBT community, even the most loving Christian can end up sounding hateful, not to mention looking, well, just plain stupid. Like it or not, the debate on what the Bible *does* and *does not* say about homosexuality is intense and personal, and it isn't going away anytime soon. Think about it: your parents and your pastor may end up communicating one thing, while your friends hold very different viewpoints. Mix in media bias and hostile voices that label Christians as intolerant, ignorant, and unenlightened, and suddenly we're up against what seems like a no-win situation.

Does this mean that we should change what we believe so we won't offend anyone?

And if we disagree with the LGBT community, are we essentially giving in to the bullies?

Is the Bible outdated and irrelevant to modern times?

Answer to each of these questions: Most definitely not!

Let's revisit the challenges we posed earlier: How should Christ-followers navigate this explosive issue. . .and handle conflicting opinions within the church?

First, regardless of the wide range of views within the Christian church, we can fully trust what the Bible says about sex, love, life, sin, death, eternity, freedom, relationships—everything—including God's plan for making us uniquely male and female. And as we study the scriptures, the Holy Spirit confirms in our hearts that it is not the word of men but the very Word of God Himself. According to popular author and pastor Joshua Harris, they are words unlike any other words on earth. "They are true and eternal," he says. "God honors those who revere and respect Him and His Word—those who treat Scripture not as mere words on a page or human invention but as the holy, God-breathed, powerful, and authoritative words of the Almighty."[1]

Second, not only should we trust God's Word, but we must stay in the battle and truly seek to *live* what we read. How? By following Christ's example and emulating love and respect for *everyone*. This means showing kindness, extending forgiveness, feeling compassion. . .and doing this for all of humanity. Every soul matters. Every human life is valuable to God.

Our Creator made humans in His image, and He pursues them with an incomprehensible passion—from the moment they're born until their very last breath. God loves you and me so much, He walked on the earth wearing skin and feeling what we feel. And then He took our sin to the cross, dying for us and giving us eternal life with Him.

God wants us to learn a thing or two about love from Christ's example. And He wants us to live it, to share it with others. True—it's easier for us to "talk a good talk" than it is to walk it, especially when we are confronted with issues that challenge what we believe. . .or when we encounter hypocrisy from those who label us as hatemongers.

So what do most of us do? We clam up and act as if we don't have an opinion, or we accidentally stick our feet in our mouths and end up just as misunderstood.

But don't lose heart.

If we trust the Bible's clear words about one man and one woman and marriage, what we've actually determined is what is good for *our* souls, right? If the Bible is God's message to humans about life and love as He originally designed, then we are responsible for our own response, our own happiness, and our own life-giving choices.

Does that make us responsible for those of others?

Are we told that we have to change other people's minds and behavior?

Are we even told whether we need to shout from the housetops about behavioral choices of others compared to ours in order to defend the character and plan of God?

Are people born with a certain sexual orientation? Can they change? Should they?

These are all good questions to talk to your parents and youth leaders about, as well as good questions to ponder as you search God's Word for answers.

LOVE WINS THE DAY

No matter what you believe and no matter how vocal you think you need to be, ultimately what Jesus would do is this: love anyone who stood before Him. Did you know that Jesus never condemned people because of their immoral behavior? (See the woman at the well in John 4 as a good example. Only He knew the woman's full story, so that is why even He didn't have to judge her.) Have you read that Jesus only got mad at religious hypocrites and not normal people trying to find their way through a very complicated life?

Yes, Jesus knows what behaviors would be good for someone's soul, but He also knows the depths of human nature—and how completely unable we are to be morally perfect. The apostle Paul knew this, too. (See Romans 7 to read what Paul had to say about how good he was.) Jesus knows that what is inside of people is more important than our outward behavior, that our hearts are evil, not just our actions. (See Matthew 5–7.) In other words, we all have an inherited sin nature, the results of which are sinful acts. (Even if a person never committed one act of sin, he or she would still need to be saved because of the sin nature.)

Would Jesus ever have shamed or ridiculed people to the

point of causing them to feel so bad about their choices—sexual or otherwise—that they might consider killing themselves as their only way out of their dilemma?

Not ever.

Yet this is what some people of faith do today. They feel it is their job to point out behaviors that run contrary to God's ideal. Why? Well, some, of course, care enough about people to want to warn them away from things that are destructive. If we really loved someone, wouldn't we, for example, want to warn them from engaging in sexual choices that could one day kill them (obtaining HIV, the virus that sometimes leads to AIDS)? Other people, of course, simply want a way to feel morally superior to prop themselves up in light of their own insecurities.

Shame and guilt do not lead to life, and rarely do they lead to a behavior change. They just lead people to conclude that Christians are mean and unloving and rarely act like Jesus. Shame and guilt set people's hearts against a loving God instead of attracting them to Him.

Does all of this mean we shouldn't have convictions about what we believe?

Does it mean we let a (sometimes) militant agenda overpower us to the point where we cower in a corner and never speak up for the "alternative" of marriage and the natural love between a man and a woman?

RESPECT WINS THE NEXT DAY

Whether a discussion on this issue occurs in class or with a group of friends, the best approach is to be respectful enough to ask questions that might get people thinking through the issue. Depending on where you are when a discussion breaks out, here are a few questions you can try:

- "If homosexuality is normal for some and not for others, and since you don't believe there is anything unique about the human race as a creation [assuming you know this about the person], then why are there only a couple of examples in the *entire* animal world of same-sex unions (e.g., certain kinds of penguins and lizards)?"
- "Could one conclude that homosexuality is a learned behavior—based on a person's background, upbringing, or thought-life—versus an inbred one? Haven't those studies on the inbred theory been challenged by mainstream scientists because the studies were thought to be biased?"
- "What other nations have viewed a sexual minority as a protected class, the way African-Americans, Hispanics, or Asians are viewed in the United States?"
- "If God created homosexuals, why didn't He openly recognize them in the Bible? 'In the beginning. . .' could have been written differently. Why, then, does He uphold marriage as the way for society?"
- "Most homosexual men have hundreds of partners in their lifetime, especially when they're younger. Doesn't their behavior show they're not interested in forming a committed relationship but only interested in pursuing pleasure?"[2]

What does the Bible say about homosexuals?

A few passages mention homosexuality directly:

Do you not know that wrongdoers will not inherit the kingdom of God? Do not be deceived: Neither the sexually immoral nor idolaters nor adulterers nor men who have sex with men nor thieves nor the greedy nor drunkards nor slanderers nor swindlers will inherit the kingdom of God. And that is what some of you were. But you were washed, you were sanctified, you were justified in the name of the Lord Jesus Christ and by the Spirit of our God.
1 CORINTHIANS 6:9–11

As you can see, homosexuality has been occurring for a long time. Whatever wonderful gifts God has created (like sex between a husband and a wife), humans have been known to corrupt. In this passage, homosexuality is lumped together with several other behaviors that God finds detestable. These are things that members of the Corinthian church *previously* practiced. But Paul makes the point that they are all forgivable deeds, doesn't he?

Paul is equally clear on what the consequences are for those who continue to practice such things. (FYI: It's unlikely that Paul would announce the consequences of his own behavior if he were homosexual. Though he did choose to remain single in order to have more freedom to spread the Gospel, he was in no way a homosexual.)

The next passage—also written by Paul—is even clearer:

> *They exchanged the truth of God for a lie, and*
> *worshiped and served created things rather than*
> *the Creator—who is forever praised. Amen.*
>
> *Because of this, God gave them over to shame-*
> *ful lusts. Even their women exchanged natural*
> *relations for unnatural ones. In the same way the*
> *men also abandoned natural relations with women*
> *and were inflamed with lust for one another. Men*
> *committed indecent acts with other men, and*
> *received in themselves the due penalty for their*
> *error. . . .*
>
> *Although they know God's righteous decree*
> *that those who do such things deserve death, they*
> *not only continue to do these very things but also*
> *approve of those who practice them.*
>
> ROMANS 1:25–27, 32

God's truth is that He created us male and female for a reason: to populate the earth, to keep us from becoming lonely, and to enable us to enjoy each other's unique differences.

If someone persists in following their own lusts—whether they feel it is a "natural attraction" or otherwise—instead of God's ideal, they are allowed to "reap what they've sown." And that includes the "acceptable sins." Unchecked gluttony will lead to obesity, heart disease, diabetes, and other natural consequences of a chosen behavior. Premarital sex could lead to pregnancy and an unplanned child. Uncontrolled anger could lead to any amount of problems that might have lifetime consequences.

God won't control a person's choices, no matter if those choices lead to a destructive conclusion. Why? He loves His creation too much to keep us as puppets. He wants us to choose to follow and obey Him, not out of fear but out of love for all that He has done.

Should you question a teacher who gives you a bad grade based on his or her personal opinions on moral issues?

Yes, as long as it's done respectfully. The student who wrote the letter at the beginning of this chapter did the right thing by going to the teacher in private and inquiring about her comments. In reality, the teacher's comments were totally out of line and subjective—at best. But she's the teacher. Unless the student decided to press the issue of the C+ and go over her head, there wasn't much more to be done.

Is Satan controlling the lives of homosexuals—and is that a good argument to use?

There's a fine line between "control" and "influence." One passage says this: "We know that we are children of God, and that the whole world is under the control of the evil one" (1 John 5:19). This is the only Bible verse that talks about what Satan has control of. It sounds like he does control those who are still living according to this world, and 2 Corinthians 4:4 backs that up: "The god of this age has blinded the minds of unbelievers, so that they cannot see the light of the gospel of the glory of Christ, who is the image of God."

In another passage, Paul says this about people who were then Christians but used to be idol worshippers: "You know that when you were pagans, somehow or other you were influenced and led astray to mute idols" (1 Corinthians 12:2). Yet it doesn't say they were controlled, does it?

Since God doesn't control a person's will, we don't believe Satan has that power either. However, if someone is not seeking God's light, he or she is susceptible to Satan's blinding influence. He plants lies in their minds, lies that turn into thoughts, attitudes, and eventually actions. He knows that taking someone deeper into a dark lifestyle—homosexual or heterosexual—is like taking them to the bottom of the sea. If you're twenty or thirty feet deep, you can still look up and see a vague light toward the surface. But if you're two hundred feet deep, you can see no light at all.

Some Christians understand this satanic strategy, but non-Christians don't. The reason: they're underwater, seeing spiritual things in a blurred fog. It's true that most unbelievers are far from the light of God's love and truth. For this reason, Satan's influence is not a good argument to use around them.

What can you say when someone has come to the wrong conclusion about Christians and how they treat practicing homosexuals?

In many parts of the country, this issue is front-page news on a weekly basis. Naturally, the liberal media portray Christians as narrow-minded hatemongers. Our worldview is that the homosexual lifestyle isn't what God intended for us (and is sometimes a deadly choice). Christians are ridiculed and accused of not being as "enlightened" as the Hollywood elite.

To be honest, some Christians *have* acted lame around unbelievers on this issue. They've said things in the wrong way or have even made hurtful statements about homosexuals to the media. That's the main reason that Christians have acquired this bad reputation. Even when we're attempting to be rational and kind, we're often lumped into this mold whether we like it or not.

Christians are in a *big* dilemma.

On the one hand, we should love, forgive, and try to help those who are caught in this sometimes deadly lifestyle. We also need to remember that we have sins of our own; and for this reason, we are commanded not to judge the motives of other human beings made in the image of God. But we are to judge their actions based on the standards of the Bible. Whereas Matthew 7:1 says, "Do not judge, or you too will be judged," verse 6 says, "Do not throw your pearls to pigs." You have to judge what the pearls are and who might not be ready to hear them. Again, only motives are not to be judged. (No one who cannot judge the actions of others in comparison to the scriptures is qualified to be a Christian leader.)

On the other hand, not only are open, practicing homosexuals tougher to reach out to, but there is within the movement a growing militancy that is fed up with what they perceive as discrimination. They want the exact same rights as heterosexuals, and they'll stoop to any tactic to attain them. In the past, organizations like ACT UP, Queer Nation, and Lesbian Avengers have been known to use intimidation and violence to make Christians (as well as the undecided) fearful of expressing their convictions.

What "rights" do they want? They want to be able to adopt children. Whether they're married or just living together, they want the same governmental privileges as any couple would receive. They want books in school libraries to portray the homosexual lifestyle as healthy and normal. Mostly they want to be looked at as a minority and thus as eligible for special rights like the physically disabled.

The problem with the LGBT desire for minority status is that they're a minority based on their sexual *preference*. If local, state, or federal governments begin to give them protected status, then they may have to continue down that path: give minority status to other groups, such as smokers, drinkers, cross-country skiers, Baptists, Catholics, and so on. The point is obvious: no one should be protected by the government on the basis of a lifestyle choice. Yet this is the radical homosexual agenda that has arrived at nearly every town and city in the country. It is extremely well funded and organized (more so than the Christian agenda).

What should the Christian response to this radical agenda be?

If we don't speak up about this powerful group, our schools and cities will crumble. If homosexuals are called a protected and abused minority, then job quotas will follow. That means that businesses (even Christian-owned businesses) will be forced to hire homosexuals in numbers proportionate to the percentage of homosexuals in the population.

The radical homosexual groups are also lobbying school boards to allow them to enter the classroom and present their case there. They want to counsel teenagers who have considered this question: "I've had *thoughts* about what it would be like to get sexual with my same sex. Does that mean I'm a homosexual?"

The answer these groups would like to present is, "Yes. . .and that's okay. You were born that way; don't fight it." This is recruiting, plain and simple.

What about the argument that homosexuals and lesbians, even "transgender" people, are born that way, that it's not just a choice? Hasn't science proved this to be true?

We have received a couple of letters in which the person writing says they have "gay feelings." That is, for a very brief time as they awaken sexually, they are more attracted to the same sex than to the opposite sex. This is common for a very small percentage of teens. If this attraction is combined with emotional or environmental factors, then a teen may continue to lean toward homosexuality.

In research for this book, we spoke with a former homosexual. He told us that's what happened to him. He felt an attraction to males, but he also said that there were other problems that pushed him in that direction. Pornography played a huge role in making him attracted to other guys. His father could not show appropriate affection for him (having been molested in childhood, and because his own father didn't know how to show him affection). At age twelve he was exposed to homosexual videos and molested by a neighbor. All along the way, he had no one with whom to talk these feelings through. He was alone.

At age twenty-one he went into the homosexual lifestyle and found that nearly every other homosexual or lesbian he met had similar influences. (The women, he said, often had been molested by a man whom they had trusted. Plus they'd had difficulty forming good relationships with boys their own age.)

He said that it all started with wrong thought patterns that could not be discussed with a trusted adult. Combined with the other factors, this pushed him over the edge.

Regarding the well-publicized argument that homosexuals are born and not made, here are the facts: much of the research that the mainstream press has reported on has been done *by* a homosexual *for* homosexuals. There simply haven't been enough credible studies done over a long enough period of time and by unbiased researchers to point to any conclusions.

So how exactly should Christian students respond when they are hit with this issue?

Since the radical end of the homosexual movement does not have widespread acceptance in the public schools like it does in much of the media, what Christian students will likely be confronted with is this:

    1. Classroom discussions in which a teacher or a few students take up "the cause."

    2. A confused—and often silent—classmate who is either "in the closet" (hiding homosexual practices, which

is more common) or open about her or his sexual choices. Christians who have thought through their responses have consulted what the Bible says about loving sinners and aren't trying to put down others in order to make themselves look good. They will usually take the high road. That is, they'll preface every comment or argument with something like the following:

"We're all human, and everyone makes choices that aren't always healthy for them. I've learned that God is very forgiving when we're able to admit that what we've done is wrong. But I can't in good conscience agree that these choices are God's best. Isn't it true that none of us would agree that the choice of sharing needles to use illegal drugs is the right choice? The virus that causes AIDS is epidemic among those who do this. So why would I say that practicing homosexuality is any better? What I'd really be saying is, 'Fine, let them do what they want; they're all going to die a horrible death anyway. They deserve what they get.'

"I may not always act like it, but I say I care for people because Jesus Christ died for them; so why would I approve of this choice that causes so many young people—whom God created—to die a slow, agonizing death?"

This can be an emotional issue. But logic can prevail—even for Christians. The logic of compassion, forgiveness, and kindness will always be the correct response on moral issues such as this.

In biblical days, Jesus touched those with leprosy, spent time with the vilest of sinners, and condemned people only if they were hypocrites. If He were here today, He'd aggressively confront the wrong He witnessed (the money changers at the temple, for example), but He'd be equally aggressive in loving those trapped in sin (for example, the woman caught in adultery in John 8).

Our advice is to go light on confrontation and heavy on love.

On Your Own

1. Look up these passages and paraphrase what they say:
> Leviticus 18:22
> Deuteronomy 23:18
> Ephesians 5:3, 5–6

2. Based on the passages you have read so far in this chapter, is homosexuality a worse sin than any other, in the eyes of God? Why? Why not?

3. Look up the following three passages. Answer yes if they apply to those who are practicing the homosexual lifestyle, no if they don't.

> John 3:16   Yes ___ No ___
> John 10:9–11   Yes ___ No ___
> Luke 23:34   Yes ___ No ___

4. Based on these passages, as well as others you have read, what does God think of those who are trapped in homosexual behavior?

5. What do you think holds Christians back from treating or accepting homosexuals the way Jesus Christ would?

With a Group

1. Look up the passages and discuss the questions in the "On Your Own" section.

2. Two of the three scriptures mentioned in the first question above come from the Old Testament. Do passages like this apply to life in your world? Why? Why not?

3. What attitudes displayed by Christians have you observed regarding homosexuals?

4. How can Christians learn to deal with their fears and prejudices on this issue?

5. What do you think is the ideal response that Christians should have toward homosexuals?

6. How about our response toward those in school who think that the only thing all Christians do is judge and condemn? What should we say? What would be the best attitude to have?

Reason 8

THERE REALLY ARE OFF-BASE BELIEFS

People Mean Well, but Sometimes
They Don't Have the Whole Picture

Snapshot 1: Two girls in first-period English have their eyes glued to the horoscope section of a popular teen magazine. They start asking for class members' birth dates so they can tell them their horoscopes.

Snapshot 2: A clerk at the mall bookstore posts a flyer advertising a "human potential" workshop.

Snapshot 3: In health class, the school nurse launches into a lecture about "holistic health" and how you really should look into it.

Snapshot 4: Your best friend catches her mom sitting on the living room floor chanting, "I am god. I am god."

Are any of these "snapshots" somewhere in your "memory album"? If you just nodded yes, then you've had a modern-day encounter with an age-old error: New Age.

Check out the following strange scenario. (Hey, it's not from the files of the *Twilight Zone*; it's actually happening to guys and girls like you all across the country!)

Orbiting the Ozone

Chris hustles into her art class and takes a seat with the other students at the worktable—just as usual. But as she pulls her sketchpad out of her backpack and glances up at the teacher, that's when it hits her: things aren't usual at all. *This is strange*, she thinks. *Verrry strange!*

The instructor is sitting in a chair facing the class. His eyes are squeezed shut and his head is tilted back. His arms and legs are crossed at the wrists and ankles, yoga-style. He slowly exhales and then takes long, deep breaths (just like a weight lifter concentrating on repetitions).

The skeptical students exchange stunned smirks and puzzled looks. Others let out sarcastic remarks.

"Is he having, like. . .a diabetic seizure or something?" someone whispers.

"More like brain meltdown," fires back another voice.

Uh-oh, what's Mr. Sullivan up to? Chris wonders. *He sometimes seems like his head is somewhere in the ozone layer, but this time—yikes!*

And the words scribbled on the chalkboard are even more bizarre:

> Meditation is man's search for understanding of the universe and his own place within it. This has led man to explore the internal world: the realm of his mind. Meditation can provide self-awareness, leading to inner peace and a sense of unity with creation.

"Okay, my future artists," the teacher says, breaking out of his trancelike state and hopping to his feet. "To those of you who thought I just lost my mind—*wrong*! I focused it. . .achieving unity and peace with creation. Now I'm ready to tackle the task at hand—artistic expression."

Chris shifts her weight and nervously taps her pencil on her sketchpad. *Somethin's seriously wrong here, Lord.*

"You see, meditation is like this tool," Mr. Sullivan says, holding up a sable hair paintbrush. He then points to his description on the chalkboard. "It enables me to unlock my true potential within. Everyone has awesome potential inside. Even you."

The teacher looks right at Chris. "We reach it only when we empty the negative thoughts swirling around upstairs. Then we can visualize the masterpieces we're going to paint."

Mr. Sullivan pops a tape into his boom box. "Before we go to work this period, I want you to give meditation a try. This will tell you how to get started."

Chris slouches in her chair and slides her sunglasses on. *Help, Lord! I can't let this stuff invade my mind. I've got to speak up. But how? And will the teacher—or anyone else—even listen?*

ULTIMATE LAME RESPONSES

- "Sorry, Teacher, but you've obviously been dipping more than just your brush in the turpentine. It's time to get out of the ozone, pal!"
- "Meditate on this, friends: Satan is leading you straight to hell. You're being deceived—*big-time!*"
- "Is the school board aware of what you're up to? Perhaps I should educate them about your *Twilight Zone* techniques."

A BETTER RESPONSE

Despite its name, the so-called New Age movement is

actually selling an incredibly ancient lie. Much of its philosophy is based on Hindu beliefs that existed long before Jesus came to save the world.

Those who buy the New Age lie will often swallow hair-raising ideas, like "Everybody is a god" or "Look inward for power and healing." But what's even scarier is that this dangerous invasion from the East is gaining thousands of converts in the West. It's also infiltrating nearly every sector of society: medicine, science, business, entertainment—even the classroom.

Even if Chris's brush with the bizarre seems a bit extreme—and even if the New Age practices aren't noticeable at your school—sooner or later you'll come into contact with New Age philosophies. And like it or not, they have found their way into the chalkboard jungle. We want to arm you with the truth so you can steer clear of the nonsense.

So what's the best approach?

Understand that your teacher isn't the deceiver. He's the deceived. He's probably doing his best to improve the educational climate in his class. He may not be religious at all but has latched onto this because it sounds good. Pray for him and be willing to ask why he's doing what he does.

If you are asked to close your eyes and concentrate, pray instead and concentrate on God's Word. In your mind, recite all the verses you know. Then ask God to change the atmosphere in your classroom. Put on the armor of God and be firm in your prayers.

The Bible is the key to defeating the enemy. Satan knows this and will try any tactic to keep you from having a quiet time with Jesus. Study Ephesians 6:10–18. It describes the tools you need to stand firm. In fact, memorize it by learning one verse a week so your "sword" will be ready at all times.

Find support from Christian teachers, your parents, your pastor, or your youth leader. Tell them what's going on in your class. The adults in your church are just as concerned as you are about New Age practices infiltrating your school.

Talk to your teacher. Respectfully point out the Eastern roots of some of the things your teacher is asking you to do. Suggest that if other religious practices—such as Bible reading and prayer—are outlawed in school, this should be, too. If necessary, join other Christian students and ask to be excused from visualizing and meditating.

Be aware. Learn what the New Age is and isn't. That's the goal of the rest of this chapter.

So Exactly How Can All This New Age Stuff Hurt?

After all, some of it sounds pretty cool. . .even in tune with Christianity. Check out these common New Age goals:

- Achieve peace, harmony, and brotherhood in a world marked by turmoil and strife.
- Get in tune with "God" and become all "he" designed you to be.
- Clear away "bad thoughts, negative emotions, and anything else that fogs up your mind," by focusing your energy on what is "good, pure, and lovely."[1]

New Age philosophies often use Christian lingo, biblical ideas and teachings, and even parts of the Bible itself. And most New

Agers don't deny the existence of Jesus Christ or that He is God's Son. On top of that, New Age ideas appeal to a hunger for spiritual experience and to the yearning for a better tomorrow. These are valid desires and worthy goals. But there's one gigantic problem for Christians: this whole movement rejects the real God of the Bible.

According to the New Age, truth is found not by reading God's Word but by looking within yourself. Whatever truth you find by looking within—New Agers claim—is the right truth for you.

Once you sort through all the positive-thinking techniques, ozone phrases, and Christian-sounding concepts, you eventually discover something dark and empty. Christian author Bill Myers puts it this way: "You discover that New Age thinking can be boiled down to one thing: it's simply a hodgepodge of demonic practices from the Eastern religions, with just enough Christianity thrown in so we'll swallow the bait. Unfortunately, it isn't until the bait goes down that people discover there's a hook buried inside."[2]

WARNING SIGNS

The following statements should serve as warning signals. The minute someone coughs out phrases like these—whether at school or at the healthy salad shop just off campus (you know, the place where you can actually eat and not have a major zit attack)—your head should explode with sirens, flare guns, bells, whistles, fireworks—*anything* that triggers this message: "WARNING: All brain cells report to battle stations. Dangerous philosophies about to enter cerebral sector."

"We are one with Mother Earth." According to New Agers, there's no separation between humanity and nature or between humans and God.

"God is an impersonal energy or force." That is the ongoing theme of Star Wars, the blockbuster movie series. Here are some other terms that are often thrown around: *life force, higher consciousness, higher self, the self, mind at large, supermind, universal mind.*

"We are all 'God' whether we recognize it or not." Many popular actors in Hollywood have bought this lie.

"Jesus was just a good teacher." Most New Agers link Jesus Christ with religious figures like Buddha and Muhammad. It's not uncommon to hear statements like, "Jesus, like many other great masters, was an ordinary man who became a master of wisdom."

"A consciousness revolution achieved through meditation unlocks the divine within." Popular programs include EST (Erhard Seminars Training), rebirthing, Silva mind control, human potential workshops, chanting, and various massage therapies. These techniques are often offshoots of Eastern religions such as Buddhism, Hinduism, and Taoism.

Tuning In to the Right Source

Popular author Josh McDowell says this about the New Age movement: "It is evidence that men and women are still making the same mistake since the Garden of Eden. The Genesis account relates how Satan, in the guise of a serpent, promised

Adam and Eve that if they ate the forbidden fruit, they would 'be like God, knowing good and evil.' But Satan, the inventor of the half-truth, lied. They did not become like God."[3]

God's Word—the Bible—blows apart New Age nonsense, with the news that Jesus, "being in very nature God, did not consider equality with God something to be used to his own advantage; rather, he made himself nothing. . . . And being found in appearance as a man, he humbled himself and became obedient to death—even death on a cross!" (Philippians 2:6–8).

In other words, the rock-solid, time-tested message of the Bible is not that people can become gods but that God became a man and died for our sins so that we can have eternal life— the ultimate good news.

NEW AGE BASICS

Now that you have a grasp on why the New Age is off-base and know the warning signals, let's arm you with the facts. Here are a few New Age basics you should be aware of:

Channeling and talking with the dead

What it's all about. Some people claim that ancient seers (or wise men) communicate with them, using their mind and body. You've probably heard about these individuals on TV talk shows.

For example, a woman in Washington state claims that a thirty-five-thousand-year-old "spiritual" teacher named Ramtha speaks through her. Some folks pay hundreds of dollars to see performances by channelers like her. (*Channeler* is another term for what the Bible calls a "medium.")

Why it's the wrong channel. This practice involves one thing: demon possession. Those who channel are not dealing with friendly little "Yodas" or E.T.–type critters who want to help them have an awesome life. These spirits are evil and use any kind of deception and dirty trick they can to gain control of a person's mind, body, and soul. A demon's goal is to separate men and women from God and to send them on a fast track straight to—you guessed it—eternal darkness (hell).

Demonic spirits always take more than they give. So tell your friends not to fool around with this stuff. Because once they invite a demon to lunch, there's a good chance it won't be leaving.

What the Bible says. "Let no one be found among you who sacrifices his son or daughter in the fire, who practices divination or sorcery, interprets omens, engages in witchcraft, or casts spells, or who is a medium or spiritist or who consults the dead. Anyone who does these things is detestable to the LORD" (Deuteronomy 18:10–12).

Reincarnation

What it's all about. People who buy this lie think that after death each person returns to an endless series of lives as different people. So if you were a good person in the past life, things are going to go better for you this time around. If you were a jerk the last time, you'll pay for it by having to come back as a bottom-of-the-heap person. Most New Agers want very much to believe this. They think it will give them another chance to live a better life or to make up for a sin they've committed.

Why it's a dead-end belief. Reincarnation is in direct opposition to the Bible. God makes it clear that we live just *one* life in our earth suits, die, and are then judged by God. And the cool thing that Christians understand is that Jesus forgives our sins—regardless of what we've done—when we repent and commit our lives to Him. He is the One who helps us live joyfully every day, even in eternity.

What the Bible says. "Man is destined to die once, and after that to face judgment" (Hebrews 9:27).

Crystals

What it's all about. Many New Agers believe that clear quartz crystals are a symbol of coming into alignment with cosmic harmony. They think that a piece of clear quartz radiates with divine white light and that by seeing, touching, wearing, using, or meditating with these crystals, one can actually work with that light in a physical form and facilitate the growth of a person's awareness.

Why crystals can't solve your problems. Think about it: spiritual awareness attained through a rock? Sounds sorta silly, doesn't it? The idea that crystals can protect or heal you is simply a lie. Whether sewn into the seam of a pair of jeans or hung in a car, a crystal is just a cool-looking rock and doesn't have any kind of power. Some teens actually carry a crystal to school, hoping it will help them do better on a test. This is foolish.

There is no biblical reason to believe in a New Age idea of psychic energy pervading the universe. Though we do believe in demonic energy that can work through occult practices, there is no reasonable basis to cause us to hold that crystals have inherent properties that make them transmitters of demonic power.

The fact is, crystals are a part of God's creation, which He pronounced good at the time He made it. There is nothing inherently occultic or spiritually dangerous about crystals, and if a Christian is interested in or attracted to them, he or she should be able to pursue this interest or attraction in good conscience.

What the Bible says. "If any of you lacks wisdom, you should ask God, who gives generously to all without finding fault, and it will be given to you" (James 1:5).

Horoscopes

What it's all about. These seemingly innocent bits of advice that appear in newspapers every day are a form of astrology, which is rooted in the New Age movement. Astrology is viewed as one of the ways to "develop your consciousness and spirituality" and "establish a means of communication with your Higher Self."[4]

Why it's a dose of bad news. According to the Bible, astrology is in the same league as channeling. . .and both are off-limits to Christians.

Humans don't have to look to the stars for answers about life or the future. We can look to the One who made them— God. Getting people to search creation for answers rather than

MICHAEL ROSS & GREG JOHNSON

ask the Creator is a deception of the devil. And according to the Word of God, horoscopes represent a doorway to a spiritual dimension that God forbids us to enter.

What the Bible says. "They are prophesying to you false visions, divinations, idolatries and the delusions of their own minds" (Jeremiah 14:14).

Occult-related games

What it's all about. On the surface, they appear to be innocent games that offer harmless fun. They come in a variety of forms: Ouija boards, crystal balls, tarot cards, and activities such as Kabala, ESP, telepathy, or Dungeons and Dragons.

Why these are the devil's toys. Each of these games has its roots in the occult. Understand that when your hands are on a Ouija board or when you cast spells during an episode of Dungeons and Dragons, you are not engaging in activities that glorify God. Play with these "toys," and you are at the mercy of the demon spirits behind them.

Instead, spend time with God and seek Him. Through Jesus you will find healing and the best life you've ever imagined. Remember, there is only one God and one mediator between God and man—Jesus Christ.

What the Bible says. "It is the LORD your God you must follow, and him you must revere. Keep his commands and obey him; serve him and hold fast to him" (Deuteronomy 13:4).

On Your Own

1. Read Genesis 3:1–7. What did Satan promise Adam and Eve if they ate the forbidden fruit?

2. Was this promise actually fulfilled when they did eat it?

3. Read Acts 14:8–18. What did these two solid missionaries do when the crowd acclaimed them as gods?

4. Jot down how you think Paul and Barnabas would have responded to the New Age belief that we can become gods by transforming our consciousness.

With a Group

1. Have you ever been in a classroom situation in which something "weird" happened?

2. Share some New Age ozone experiences you've had outside the classroom (like at the mall, the doctor's office, etc.).

3. Discuss what is most dangerous about the New Age movement.

4. Why should Christians not fear the power behind it?

5. What's the best way you can respond to the New Age (and steer others from this deadly trap)?

Reason 9

LIFE ALWAYS MATTERS, AND
IT'S VALUABLE AT EVERY AGE AND STAGE

Andy Pottenger's heart was racing full throttle, and his stomach felt like a toxic waste dump.

The frantic sixteen-year-old was about to stand before the firing squad in fifth-period speech—and attempt to say something intelligent.

His assignment: Go head-to-head with another student and debate abortion. Andy would make a pro-life case in favor of unborn babies.

His opponent: Nicole Swan, Central High's student body president (gorgeous, popular, voted "most likely to succeed," a straight-A student, and—*gulp!*—a convincing speaker).

Andy had a reputation for being pro-life, ever since a news crew filmed him and his youth group praying outside an abortion clinic. But when his speech teacher insisted his final project be a debate, Andy came down with a major case of the jitters.

I'm no expert! he thought. *What on earth have I gotten myself into?*

KELLIE'S HISTORY LESSON

Kellie scrunched into a tiny ball and rested her chin on her knee. The conversation between her history student partners was almost too much to handle.

"Are you sure, Holly?" Danielle pressed. "I mean, you could be a little late because of midterms. . .stress, stuff like that."

"Look, I'm not just a *little* late. Trust me, I know what's happening inside my own body." Holly put her hand on her stomach and looked down. "I'm about fourteen weeks along."

"Have you told your parents?" Melanie asked.

"Are you kidding? They'd freak."

"How about. . .him?" Danielle added.

Holly shook her head. "No."

A stabbing pain shot through Kellie's stomach as she listened. As a Christian, she couldn't imagine facing such a hard dilemma. But what she heard next nearly made her blood boil.

"We have a health clinic right here on campus," Danielle said. "They can tell you where to go to—you know—take care of it."

"And they won't tell your parents," Melanie said.

"I heard it's a pretty simple procedure," Danielle added. "They remove a bunch of cells and tissue. . .and in five minutes, it's over."

Kellie sat up and gulped. *It's a child,* she thought, *not a wart. They want to vacuum up a human like a piece of trash!*

"Did you have something to add?" Danielle asked, looking right at Kellie.

"Yeah, you've been so quiet. Speak up!" Melanie barked.

Kellie looked at Holly and swallowed. "Well, uh. . .I just feel that. . ."

What can I say. . .without them thinking that I'm some kinda religious geek? I know *what I feel inside—I just can't put it into words.*

Notice how life is full of certain touchy topics? Supersensitive subjects that generate explosions of volcanic emotion, endless arguments, warring camps.

Abortion is one of them.

Dr. James Dobson once said, "It's interesting to note. . .that a woman who plans to terminate a pregnancy usually refers to the life within her as 'the fetus.' But if she intends to deliver and love and care for the little child, she affectionately calls him 'my baby.' The need for this distinction is obvious. If we are going to kill a human being without experiencing guilt, we must first strip it of worth and dignity. We must give it a clinical name that denies its personhood."[1]

Some say we should define human life by age, believing that the bulge in the mom's stomach isn't really a baby but "fetal tissue." Does this mean that if people are too old, it's okay to get rid of them, too?

Some say we should make sure that all babies are "normal" before they're considered human (we should abort those with Down syndrome, for example). Does this mean babies with genetic deformities (like sickle-cell anemia) can be declared non-human?

Some say you have to be wanted by someone before you qualify for membership in the human race. Do we then search the country and wipe out the people no one wants—such as child abusers?

Let's assume you're convinced that abortion is (a) illogical or (b) scripturally wrong. What in the world can you do about it? How do you lead your friends in the right direction, and exactly what do you say?

Ultimate Lame Responses

- "You call yourself 'pro-choice'? Gimme a break! You people are nothing but *murderers*. . .baby killers. . .heartless spawn of Satan!"
- "Uh. . .I haven't yet formed an opinion about abortion. Sure, I'm a Christian—and my pastor says it's wrong—but I just don't know. I think there are plenty of good arguments on both sides. So I guess I'm kinda 'middle of the road.' "
- "Personally, I'm against abortion. . .but just do whatever *you* think is best. Hey, I won't step on your toes with *my* values."

A Better Response

The key is to defuse the bomb (human emotion) and present the facts. Impossible? Not if you do these things:

- Know what you believe and *why* you believe it.
- Don't argue but instead stay calm and confidently reveal the truth.
- Dispel the myths and show how many pro-abortion arguments are manipulative, unreasonable, and callous to the truth.

Let's sit in on Andy's big speech to see if he is able to turn the tide of "politically correct" pro-abortion hype.

The Classroom Debate

Nicole kicked off the action, blasting away with several popular arguments for abortion.

"A woman has the right to privacy over her own body," she insisted. "*No one* should ever take that away. What happens in a clinic is solely the business of a woman and her doctor."

Nicole paused, tossed back her long brunette hair, then locked eyes with Andy. "Just what are those antiabortionists trying to prove, anyway?

"They distort the truth and tug at our emotions," she added. "They show us ghastly photos of nonbreathing fetuses in buckets and try to make the pro-choice side look like heartless butchers."

A few howls rose from the class. Andy slid down in his seat and nervously fumbled through his notes. *I'm definitely lunchmeat!* he thought, panicking.

"An abortion is a safe and simple medical procedure that doesn't murder a baby," Nicole continued. "It merely puts an end to an unwanted pregnancy."

Let's review the facts

Without even looking at her notes, Nicole then launched into her speech:

"The fetus is an extension of the pregnant woman's body, like her teeth or tonsils.

"Since the unborn is nothing more than a bunch of tissue, abortion ends a pregnancy. It doesn't kill a baby.

"The fetus isn't yet a complete human being. It's more like a blueprint for a potential baby, not an actual one.

"Life begins at birth. That's why we celebrate birthdays, not conception days.

"Every woman has a right to reproductive freedom, especially control over her own body. That's why we must preserve our right to choose.

"If abortion is made illegal, thousands of women will lose their lives to rusty clothes hangers in back alleys.

"The unborn isn't a person with meaningful life. It can't even think and is less advanced than an animal.

"It's wrong to bring an unwanted baby into this world. The child will probably end up unloved and abandoned."

Nicole's final punch

After walking the class through these key pro-choice points, Nicole pulled out the heavy artillery and ended her speech with a jolt: "What about a woman whose unborn baby is diagnosed as being deformed or handicapped?" she asked. "What about a woman who is pregnant due to rape or incest? Isn't it more cruel to force her to have the baby than to end the pregnancy. . .and erase the horrible memory?

"That radical minority that calls itself pro-life can't shove their religious beliefs down our throats," Nicole concluded. "And we can't let them step all over our right to free choice."

The room thundered with applause. Nearly everyone clapped and howled their support.

Nicole walked past Andy and smiled. "Good luck, Pottenger. You'll need it!"

*"If we accept that a mother can kill even her own child,
how can we tell other people not to kill each other? . . .
Any country that accepts abortion is not teaching its people
to love but to use any violence to get what they want."*
MOTHER TERESA

A den of lions

It was Andy's turn now, and it was almost as if fifth-period speech had transformed from a safe classroom to a dangerous jungle—filled with fierce predators.

As he looked out at his classmates, the football-sized hands of the school's quarterback, who was sitting in the front row, suddenly looked more like the deadly paws of a husky lion. Even the teacher's tall, fluffy beehive resembled the matted mane of the king of beasts.

Andy swallowed and squeezed his eyes shut. *Lord, they're gonna pounce on every word and chew up every idea,* he prayed silently. *I'm in a den of lions. . . . Help!*

"And now, class, we'll hear an *anti*abortion argument from Andy Pottenger," the teacher announced.

Andy took his place behind the podium and scanned the crowded classroom. His knees shook and his mouth felt like it was full of peanut butter. But he tried to concentrate on all the stuff his youth pastor had taught him—and all the spine-chilling photos he had seen.

It's up to me to set the facts straight, he thought.

A Reason to Abort?

One doctor said to another, "I would like your opinion
about the termination of a pregnancy. The father has
syphilis. The mother has tuberculosis. Of their first four
children born, the first was blind, the second died,
the third was deaf and dumb, the fourth also had
tuberculosis. What would you have done?"
"I would have ended the pregnancy," said the second doctor.
"Then you would have murdered Beethoven."
P. B. MEDAWAR, *LIFE OR DEATH: ETHICS AND OPTIONS*

Truth is truth

"Nicole bombarded us with point after point about women's
rights and free choice," Andy said. "But she completely missed
what's *really* at stake: a living, functioning *human life*."

A few groans rose from the crowd. Andy gripped the podium and focused on his notes. "Abortionists blast pro-lifers for
showing photos of dead babies in buckets, claiming we're distorting fact with cheap theatrics.

"But truth is truth: *dead babies who are discarded are exactly
what abortion amounts to. Every abortion stops a beating heart.*"

Let's review the facts

Andy's last statement made a few heads pop up, but he knew
he faced an uphill battle. So he stepped to the side of the podium and tried to make eye contact with each kid in class as he
continued his speech:

"*A fetus is* not *just another part of a woman's body.* A body part is defined by the common genetic code it shares with the rest of its body. The unborn's genetic code differs from the mother's, even to the extent that some unborn babies are male, while their moms are female.

"*An unborn human is* not *just a blob of tissue.* From the moment of conception, the unborn is what it is. . .a separate, *living* human being. At six weeks, you can see a beating heart. At twelve weeks, eyes and hands can be observed.

"*A fetus is* not *just a blueprint or a potential human.* A fetus is a person at a particular stage of development—much like a toddler or an adolescent. The fact is, something nonhuman does not become human by getting older and bigger.

"*Life does* not *begin at birth.* Science has shown us that human life begins at conception. All genetic characteristics of a distinct individual are present from the moment of conception. Our recognition of birthdays is cultural, not scientific.

"*Denying abortion does* not *step all over a woman's rights and freedoms.* The onetime choice of abortion robs someone else of a lifetime of choices and creates pain for the mother, not to mention others involved. Furthermore, responsible societies *must* deny choices that would harm others.

"*If abortion is made illegal, thousands of women will* not *die from rusty clothes hangers.* Prior to the legalization of abortion, 90 percent of abortions were done not in back alleys but by physicians in their offices. In fact, women in America still die from *legal* abortions.

"*The early stage of human life* is *as meaningful as any other stage.* But if we listened to abortionists, who base human value on size and intelligence, then we'd also have to dehumanize other members of society: dwarfs, basketball centers, the obese, the mentally disabled. And when we dehumanize the beginning of life, we dehumanize the end of it as well.

"*Since human life is valuable, every human is wanted.* A pregnancy may be unwanted, but there is no such thing as an unwanted child. The list of couples wanting to adopt runs into the millions. And if we destroy all human beings we believe are 'unwanted,' then *any* segment of society is at risk: AIDS victims, the elderly, derelicts, et cetera."

Andy's Final Punch

"Using phrases like 'terminating a pregnancy' may sound better, but the fact is that abortion is deadly. Every abortion stops a beating heart and terminates measurable brain waves."

The entire class sat perfectly still. The snide smirks and rolling eyes had turned to blank stares. Nicole looked bored and occasionally glanced out the window or scribbled little circles on her algebra book cover.

Andy stepped away from the podium and delivered *his* knockout blow: "Americans kill nearly one and a half million unborn babies a year through abortion," he explained. "That's more than four thousand a day, or one about every twenty seconds.

"Hitler killed six million Jews," Andy continued. "But since 1973, Americans have exterminated more than 56 million unborn babies. No matter what some believe, the truth is that abortion kills. . .*and that's wrong.*"

As Andy closed, the fierce lions in fifth-period speech began to look a lot more like purring house cats. But even if he hadn't changed everyone's mind, Andy had set the facts straight—and had done his part to idiot-proof the pro-life message.

GRUESOME STATS

- Fifty-six million abortions have been performed in the United States since 1973.
- By the time you finish reading this chapter, thirty babies will have been aborted. An abortion is performed in this country every twenty seconds—an estimated forty-three hundred per day.
- Nearly two hundred thousand second- and third-trimester abortions are performed annually—seventeen thousand of those occur after five months of pregnancy.
- Nearly half of all women obtaining abortions admit to not using any method of birth control during the month that they became pregnant.
- The abortion industry is a business that is estimated to generate $400 million a year.[2]

HOW ABORTIONS ARE DONE

Suction aspiration. Ninety percent of all abortions involve the use of a high-powered vacuum that is inserted in the womb. Its purpose is to suck the baby out into a container so it can be dumped.

Dilation and curettage. Here a loop-shaped knife is inserted to cut the baby apart; the pieces are scraped out through the cervix.

Dilation and evacuation. A grasping forceps (similar to pliers with teeth) is inserted into the womb to tear apart the baby one piece at a time.

Saline injection. A concentrated salt solution is injected into the womb. The baby swallows the solution and usually dies one to two hours later from burned-out lungs, dehydration, brain hemorrhaging, and convulsions.

On Your Own

1. Think about it. Doctors say that just twenty-eight days after conception, a half-inch long human fetus has a developing brain as well as a beating heart. With this in mind, check out Psalm 139:13, 15–16.

2. Now complete the following:
   - Psalm 139 makes it clear that a fetus is not simply "a mass of tissue" or a "potential life" because. . .
   - Abortion is not an option for Christians because. . .

3. List three things that are unique about you (talents, abilities, strengths).
   -
   -
   -

4. For a moment, imagine that you had been aborted. If you weren't in the picture today, how would your family be different? What would your friends be like? (Think of some ways in which your life has impacted the lives of others.)

5. Read 1 Corinthians 6:19–20. Based on this passage, answer the following:

- Has God given us absolute ownership of our bodies?
- How does this scripture passage affect the argument that a woman should have "control over her body" and "the right to choose abortion"?

With a Group

1. Some pro-abortion Christians claim that since the Bible does not specifically condemn it, abortion must not be wrong. Take a look at these scripture passages: Job 31:15; Psalm 139:13; Jeremiah 1:4–5; and Luke 1:44.

- When does human life begin, at conception or at birth?
- What do the scriptures say about the sanctity of human life?
- Is abortion murder?

2. You may have heard an argument that goes something like this: "The preborn are not fully human. Therefore it's not morally wrong to terminate a 'potential life.' " Check out Judges 13:3, 6–7; Isaiah 49:1; and Jeremiah 1:5.

- What do these passages say about the humanity of the

preborn?

- Based on these scripture passages—as well as the information presented in this chapter—do humans become individuals at conception or at birth?

3. Read Job 12:10. If God is the author of life, can abortion ever be an option? Can you cite a situation in which you think abortion might be okay?

4. Let's plunge ahead ten years into the future.

Suppose this happens:

- You and your spouse are sitting in a doctor's office. The physician leans forward and looks you directly in the eye. "I have bad news. Your child is otherwise healthy, but our tests show that it hasn't developed legs or a right arm. And there's a chance it could be brain-damaged. If you wish, we can terminate the pregnancy right now."
- How would you react? What would you do?

Reason 10

UNREALITY CAN'T WIN

We know you're ready to get the book over with. But there's one more very important thing to talk about.

If you've ever known a bank teller, they will tell you they are taught one essential skill: the ability to spot the real from the counterfeit. Even though fake money is rare, it's also extremely illegal. So bank personnel are shown the difference between a real bill and a fake one. They can tell by sight, by feel, even by smell, what is real and what is not.

Though the issues we've covered so far may not apply to *everyone* reading these pages, one thing we've learned from our years of being teenagers—and our years of working with them— is this: unreality and the counterfeit life love to take up residence in the mind of a teen—even a Christian teen.

What kind of unreality do we want to end with? Well, it's different for girls and guys. It seems each gender has a tendency to glue themselves onto their own unique type of fantasy. And guys and gals sometimes get stuck in unreality.

Before we talk about what it tends to be for each sex, a word about fantasy.

First, there's the harmless variety.

For example, dreaming of being an airplane pilot, a pro athlete, president of the United States, an Olympic champion, a war hero, a doctor or nurse, a missionary or pastor—these are all safe fantasies. Safe because, to a degree, they are all possible. That is, most are goals worth dreaming about. Fantasizing about what it would be like to one day dunk over a 7-foot 4-inch NBA center may not get you into pro ball, but it may motivate you to work toward that athletic dream, it may lead to a college scholarship, or it may plant within you a hunger to teach or coach.

What starts as a childhood dream often leads to a very fulfilling career.

Then there's the not-so-harmless variety.

Christian idiots are made, not born. The enemy has a long track record of success in slowly polluting the mind of the young Christian. It's not childish, childhood fantasies he wants young believers to dream about; it's adult-type, potentially lifetime addiction to unreality he wants Christians to swallow.

Satan starts by planting seeds early in a person's life. He waters these seeds through repetitive temptations until they begin to sprout. Then he sits back and watches as one of them grows so large it consumes the once pure and naive follower of Christ.

He attacks us in our weakest areas, and these areas are different for girls and guys.

FOR GIRLS IT'S THE HUNGER FOR ROMANCE

Disney, of course, has known this for decades. *Sleeping Beauty*, *Cinderella*, *The Little Mermaid*, and other movies present girls as able to be happy and fulfilled only if they have a man to call their own. And once they have one, their life is complete.

Since TV began, afternoon and nighttime soap operas have daily kept the romantic fires burning for teenage girls, housewives, and working women (those who have DVRs). For some, knowing the love life of their favorite characters borders on obsession.

Also on the list of romance inducers are the hundreds of "romance novels" that girls read. I (Greg) once knew a Christian girl who would read two or three per week. At age nineteen she thought she had met her handsome hero. A man in the service swept her off her feet, and they were married in less than two months.

Were her romantic dreams fulfilled? Not even close. The first week of marriage was a nightmare as they traveled to his next post of duty. For three months, they lived in a mobile home while he went to work every day. When she realized that her man wasn't the one she had been fantasizing about, she sought—and got—an annulment. The marriage was over.

Two years later, she thought she had found her *real* lifetime lover. He was a strong Christian, too. Within a year she had divorced him. Not able to handle the guilt, she completely ditched her once-strong faith in pursuit of the ideal guy. The bar scene is where she ended up, going from one guy to the next.

Extreme story, you think? Perhaps. But maybe not. The more likely scenario that Satan orchestrates happens something like this: Thoughts that a man is the answer to a girl's life are fueled through the sources just mentioned. She finds a man who loves her and treats her right. They get engaged, get married, start a home, begin to have kids. . . Everything is perfect, right? Just like the movies. Except that what happens is that the man gets busy with work, she gets busy with work or the kids, and pretty soon, familiarity breeds contempt. The handsome prince turns out to be a normal guy and the pressures of daily survival make her wonder if she's missed something along the way.

Perhaps there's a better life out there somewhere, she thinks.

Millions of women—Christian women—have these thoughts. (Go ahead, ask a few.) But instead of leaving their family and running away with someone else, most (but not all) simply stay married and try to survive their unfulfilled expectations about men and romance.

Romance is great. Marriage *is* wonderful. Some men do turn out to be quality guys. But when a girl places unreal expectations on a member of the male species—ideas that he has the ability to endlessly fulfill the romantic fantasies of his mate—her dreams *will* be shattered. Only one man ever promised to bring "life in all its fullness" to us humans (male and female): Jesus Christ. Nowhere does the Bible promise that a man will make a woman's life complete. The reason is because it's an unreal expectation. It can't happen.

Ah, but that's not what soap operas, movies, and novels say, right?

FOR GUYS IT'S AN ILLICIT ATTRACTION TO THE OPPOSITE SEX

Illicit means improper, prohibited, unlawful, or unauthorized.

You may not have been aware that there's an alarm clock built into every guy. At the right point in our maturity, it goes off. We open our eyes, shake our heads, and say, "Girls are different! Good job, God!"

For each guy, that alarm clock goes off at a different time (usually between the ages of eleven and fifteen). Those feelings are nothing we can conjure up or manufacture. God gave them to us; they're normal, right, and really one of God's best ideas.

Waking up to females is what we call an *innocent* attraction. It's a wonderful realization. But what happens with guys about this same time isn't so wonderful. Satan tries everything he can to take the wonder and innocence out and put obsession and illicitness in. What fuels a male's obsession? It's different for each guy, but here are a few places where it begins:

- Friends at school start talking about body parts. (We've already covered this one, so we won't talk about this subject again.)
- TV shows or commercials not only talk about it; they also reveal a lot more skin than you'd *ever* see—unless you lived at the beach.
- Ditto for movies—even the covers of videos are provocative.
- Billboards.
- Swimsuit issues in male sports magazines.
- Last, and certainly most, Internet porn.

This last point is the place Satan wants all the other things to lead to, guys (and some girls). His strategy is to take the normal, innocent attraction of what's reality for guys and turn it into an illicit obsession in unrealityland. He's patient but unrelenting. Viewing pictures or streaming videos of naked women keeps *Christian* men—by the thousands—frustrated, guilt-ridden, and unable to live in reality as it relates to the true desires of the female in their life.

Plus it's addictive. That's right. Like any drug, pornography is progressive; the more you look, the more you want. It actually makes the brain secrete the same hormone—dopamine—that cocaine does. If you don't believe porn can be as addictive as cocaine, you have your head in the proverbial sand. And the other sad truth is you'll soon want different, increasingly disgusting or violent forms of porn to get the same rush.

It's beyond the scope of this book to detail to someone who is already hooked by this stuff how to get off it. Our goal is to make you aware that this seed Satan sows into the mind of a man is the most destructive and fastest-growing seed the enemy plants. Once in bloom, it fuels unreal thoughts about sex, thoughts that can severely hinder the lifetime of enjoyment God wants you to have with one woman for the rest of your life.

Yes, that's a pretty heavy statement, but it's true. If you don't believe us, show these words to a trusted adult and ask him how many men he knows—older men in their thirties and forties—who are still in bondage to this stuff. We're not blowing smoke on this one, guys. There are Christian male sex addicts in our churches, and their sickness didn't just happen to start in their post-teenage years. For most, it started "innocently" or "accidentally." They found pornographic material on their smart phones or even on their parents' home computers or a friend's dad's DVD "collection." Pornography is everywhere.

If you haven't allowed your eyes to feast on this stuff as of yet—or if you've just looked a few times—we challenge you to make perhaps the toughest commitment of your life: commit to *never* willingly gaze at this stuff for as long as you live. If there's a "life mission" that a man must have, it's to keep his mind pure from images that will rob him of the wonder of experiencing sex the way God intended: with a lifetime wife. This challenge is for boys who really want to become Christian men.

BACK TO REALITY

Enjoying life to its fullest means living in reality, not fantasy. Christian idiocy occurs when the teenage believer fails to recognize the seeds Satan is trying to sow during these adolescent years.

This is one area where the Christian teen likely *won't* look like a geek during his or her teenage years. The consequences of living in unreality won't occur until later in life. But the potential for long-term unhappiness is incredible. Many adults' downward spiral didn't begin in their twenties; it began during their teens.

Please! Don't let that downward spiral begin during your teen years. Live in reality today, and you'll enjoy the reality God wants to give you the rest of your life.

On Your Own

1. Rank the other areas where people at your school try to live in unreality:

___ Gambling

___ Pursuing unrealistic goals

___ Drinking

___ Fantasy role-playing games

___ Drugs

___ Other

2. What do these passages say about the real kingdom Jesus is from?

> Matthew 26:53
>
> John 6:15
>
> John 18:36

3. Living in unreality means being in the dark when it comes to living in reality. What do these passages say about what God wants to do with those who live in darkness?

> Luke 1:77–79
>
> John 12:46
>
> 1 Peter 2:9

4. What are people naturally attracted to?

> John 3:19
>
> John 7:7

5. What happens when we walk in darkness?

> John 12:35–36

With a Group

1. Answer the questions above.

2. Why do you think people walk into the world of unreality?

3. What can you do for a pre-Christian you know who is living in an unreal or fantasy world?

4. What can you do when you see a Christian living in unreality?

5. What is the best way you can identify reality so you don't drift into the world of unreality?

☞ Extra Stuff #1
Resolving "Contradictions" in the Bible

Ronald Youngblood[1]

The next time someone asks you about a contradiction in the Bible, you can be prepared to give an answer.

Several years ago when I was an interim pastor, a member of my congregation came to my office greatly agitated. He'd learned that a seminary instructor had said some numbers in the Old Testament are simply estimates, and he was concerned that this cast doubt on the Bible's inerrancy.

The verse in question had to do with a battle in Judges 20:46, for which the casualty count is given as 25,000.

I asked, "Don't you think 25,000 could have been a round number—that the count was somewhere between 23,000 and 27,000?"

My friend insisted this couldn't be so.

"Well, what would be reasonable from your standpoint?" I asked. "That it was somewhere between 24,000 and 26,000?"

"No."

"Somewhere between 24,990 and 25,010?"

"No.

"How about between 24,999 and 25,001?" I asked. "Or are you saying it has to be right on the money?"

"Well. . .yes."

In those days, the war in Vietnam was in the news daily. "The casualty counts in the newspapers are obviously estimates. Why can't it be that way in the Bible?" I asked.

"Because the daily paper isn't my Bible," he replied.

"Good enough. But what if I showed you two verses in the Old Testament, both describing the same incident, where different figures are used?" I asked.

"Is that right? Are there such passages?"

At this point, I showed him the story of King David's census of fighting men, which is recorded twice: in 2 Samuel 24 and in 1 Chronicles 21. In the first account, Joab reports to the king: "In Israel there were eight hundred thousand able-bodied men who could handle a sword, and in Judah five hundred thousand" (verse 9).

This 1.3 million total in Samuel does not square precisely with the same story in Chronicles. There Joab reports a different number of men to David: "In all Israel there were one million one hundred thousand men who could handle a sword, including four hundred seventy thousand in Judah" (verse 5).

When we closed the Bible, my friend sighed with relief. "I'm glad we've talked," he said. "It takes a big weight off my shoulders. I'd always wondered why counts in the Bible come out in round numbers so often."

I think of my friend when I encounter other Christians who are disturbed by similar apparent discrepancies in scripture. Sometimes, simple explanations can relieve the concern over verses that are puzzling or seem to contradict each other.

Another possible explanation for numerical discrepancies

(in addition to "rounding off") is that a transcriber made an error when transcribing from an earlier manuscript. (In 1 Samuel 13:1 the numbers giving the length of Saul's reign seem to have been dropped from the Hebrew text.) I believe the original writers' work was inerrant. Those copying it, however, were subject to the kinds of human errors even the most thorough and dedicated scribes can make.

Using a good study Bible can resolve many such worries. And it can help Christians defuse the arguments of skeptics who delight in pointing to apparent contradictions as evidence that the Bible should be read as fiction or mythology: "If the Bible is the Word of God, why do some passages contradict others?" Let's examine eight such instances so we can respond.

DAVID'S INSPIRATION TO TAKE A CENSUS OF ISRAELITE TROOPS

Going back to the two passages we looked at earlier, in 2 Samuel and 1 Chronicles, we find not only the discrepancy in numbers but also a "contradiction" regarding who incited David to take the census:

"The anger of the LORD burned against Israel, and [the LORD] incited David" (2 Samuel 24:1) and "Satan rose up against Israel and incited David" (1 Chronicles 21:1).

Is this a gross contradiction or an equating of God and Satan?

It's neither. Scripture is clear that God does not cause anyone to sin (James 1:13). It's also clear that man's—and Satan's—evil acts are under God's sovereign control (Judges 3:7–11; Job 1:12; 2:6; 1 Corinthians 10:13). Satan caused the action, but God allowed it. The writer of 2 Samuel, perhaps out of reverence, was led to credit God Himself as the ultimate cause.

THE FEEDING OF FIVE THOUSAND AND THE FEEDING OF FOUR THOUSAND

Some people are troubled by what they see as contradictions in the numbers of people who were fed loaves and fish at one event. The explanation is simple: Mark is describing separate occasions.

By reading carefully through the two passages (Mark 6:30–44; 8:1–10), we can see how the details of the incidents differ. In the earlier account, Jesus was met by a crowd on the shore after He had been with His disciples in a boat. In the later incident, the crowd had been with Jesus for three days.

Moreover, different numbers of loaves and fishes were divided on the two occasions. Jesus discusses these as two separate incidents in Mark 8:18–20:

> *"And don't you remember? When I broke the five loaves for the five thousand, how many basketfuls of pieces did you pick up?"*
>
> *"Twelve," they replied.*
>
> *"And when I broke the seven loaves for the four thousand, how many basketfuls of pieces did you pick up?"*
>
> *They answered, "Seven."*

TWO PROVERBS THAT APPEAR TO GIVE CONTRADICTORY ADVICE

Proverbs 26:4 says, "Do not answer a fool according to his folly, or you yourself will be just like him," but the very next verse says, "Answer a fool according to his folly, or he will be wise in his own eyes."

Are we to answer the fool or not?

Each situation requires a judgment call, the inspired writer is saying. On one hand, if you answer a fool according to his folly, you may be stooping to his level. On the other hand, if you don't, he may think he is wise, and you will have missed an opportunity to denounce his foolishness.

There is no perfect solution when dealing with a fool. Here are two suggestions (not ironclad rules). A believer must discern which is applicable in different situations.

It's important to understand the source of proverbs and how they should be read. The wise men or sages associated with the wisdom books were an important force in Israelite society (Jeremiah 18:18). They were called on to give advice to kings and also to instruct the young.

While prophets tended to deal with the religious side of life, the wise men were concerned about everyday matters. Therefore we must not interpret the book of Proverbs as prophecy or its statements about certain cause-and-effect relationships as promises.

The situation is somewhat akin to maxims your grandmother might have given you. "A stitch in time saves nine," she'd sometimes say, admonishing you not to delay. But at other times she'd warn, "Haste makes waste." This conflicting advice didn't cause a problem, because you understood Granny's common sense. Either motto might be appropriate in a given circumstance.

THE NUMBER OF WOMEN WHO WENT TO THE TOMB OF THE RESURRECTED JESUS

Because each Gospel gives a detailed description of the events surrounding Jesus' crucifixion, burial, and resurrection, they present some of the most fascinating instances of alleged discrepancies in scripture. To take a single example: Did one woman (John 20:1), two (Matthew 28:1), three (Mark 16:1), or five or more (Luke 24:10) go to the empty tomb on that first Easter Sunday morning?

First, we observe that none of the Gospel writers insists that the woman (women) he mentions was (were) the only one (ones) present. In fact, John implies that Mary Magdalene was not alone, because he quotes her as saying, concerning Jesus, "We don't know where they have put him!" (John 20:2).

It's entirely possible that the women came to the tomb at various times and from various places in the city so they would not arouse suspicion or attract attention. We should not assume that they all came at once or from the same place.

Perhaps Mary Magdalene went to the tomb first (as recorded by John). She was soon joined by Mary the mother of James (as Matthew implies), then by Salome (Mark's account), and finally by Joanna and one or more other women (Luke's Gospel). Such a reconstruction accounts for the differences without needlessly turning them into contradictions.

ACCOUNTS IN JOSHUA OF ISRAEL'S CONQUEST OF CANAAN THAT SEEM TO BE CONTRADICTED IN JUDGES

Joshua tells of the blitzkrieg conquest of Canaan. It presents an optimistic picture of what took place during six years (at most) as it relates the series of victories—in central, southern, and northern Canaan—that gave the Israelites control of all the hill country and the Negev.

Then we open the book of Judges, which indicates things were not as rosy as they first seemed. Chapters 1 and 2 describe mopping-up operations and then give us a list of towns that were not taken because the conquerors were sinful.

Why these differing accounts? It has to do with the way things appeared at the times the books were written.

The discussion in Joshua of the conquest of the land was accurate—as far as it went. It was only later, at the time of Judges, that pockets of resistance were found. The earlier conquest was as complete as it needed to be (Joshua), but some towns had to be recaptured later on (Judges).

Two Accounts of Judas's Suicide

According to Matthew 27:5, Judas "went away and hanged himself," but in Acts 1:18 we read that he "fell headlong, his body burst open and all his intestines spilled out."

This is an example of an apparent contradiction we can resolve with an understanding of biblical culture and the ways that words are translated.

In our culture, "hanging from a tree" suggests a scene from a TV western in which a lynch mob puts a noose around someone's neck. The victim is killed by strangulation, "hanging from a tree."

But this was not a form of execution in biblical times; the

MICHAEL ROSS & GREG JOHNSON

common method was impaling on a post. Following impalement, the body would be displayed as a warning to others.

To understand the story of Judas's suicide, we must know what its key words signified. The word *hanged* meant "impaled," and *tree* was a wooden pole on which the body was hung after execution.

Even the New Testament reference to Christ's crucifixion "Cursed is everyone who is hung on a pole" (Galatians 3:13) was talking about hanging as a form of impaling (spikes were driven into Christ's body). And what some versions refer to as a "tree" was the wooden pole, or cross.

So the two accounts of Judas's death are not at odds. It seems his "hanging" was an impalement caused when he jumped (or fell) onto a sharpened post.

For thousands of years, scripture has proved itself to be totally trustworthy and absolutely authoritative. The burden of proof, then, is on the person claiming to find a contradiction, who must demonstrate that it has no reasonable explanation.

And for believers, discovering possible explanations for these "contradictions" can lead to greater understanding, appreciation, and conviction concerning the Bible.

☞ Extra Stuff #2
Power Up Daily

A Radical Way to Study Scripture

1. Receive God's Word

We genuinely receive the Word of God into our minds by reading, listening to, and "spiritually consuming" the words of the Bible.

Eugene H. Peterson is a Bible scholar who spent a big part of his life translating scripture into a user-friendly version we know as *The Message.* Take a look at what he says about receiving scripture into our minds: "Words spoken or written to us under the metaphor of eating, words to be freely taken in, tasted, chewed, savored, swallowed, and digested, have a very different effect on us from those that come at us from the outside, whether in the form of propaganda or information."[1] In other words, receiving scripture is much more than an information-gathering pursuit. In fact, Bible study alone will not give us eternal life. Remember the Pharisees in Jesus' day? They often memorized entire texts, yet they failed to experience the truths found in God's Word. "It is a subtle temptation to prefer the book to the Author," Henry T. Blackaby warns. "A book will not confront you about your sin; the Author will. Books can be ignored; it is much harder to avoid the Author when He is seeking a relationship with you."[2]

The Power by Four method we introduce here is all about metabolizing God's life-giving words. We allow His message to become ours; we invite His life to surge through us. The goal is to know Jesus better, to walk with Him, to become like Him—to have a deeper relationship with Him. The scriptures help us to do this.

"When we engage the Scriptures for spiritual transformation. . .we engage not only our mind but also our heart, our emotions, our body, our curiosity, our imagination and our will," writes author Ruth Haley Barton. "We open ourselves to a deeper level of understanding and insight that grows out of and leads us deeper into our personal relationship with the One behind the text. And it is in the context of relational intimacy that real life change takes place."[3]

2. REFLECT ON GOD'S WORD

We actively reflect, think, meditate, and ponder the words of the Bible into our hearts and souls.

Not only is reflection (or meditation) an active consideration of biblical truth; it is also commanded by God. Romans 12:2 tells us, "Be transformed by the renewing of your mind. Then you will be able to test and approve what God's will is—his good, pleasing and perfect will."

Reflection fosters understanding, and understanding enables us to hear God's personal message to each one of us. Let me (Mike) demonstrate what I mean with an example. Take a close look at Christ's words in Luke 6:46–49:

> *"Why do you call me, 'Lord, Lord,' and do not do
> what I say? As for everyone who comes to me and
> hears my words and puts them into practice, I will
> show you what they are like. They are like a man*

building a house, who dug down deep and laid the foundation on rock. When a flood came, the torrent struck that house but could not shake it, because it was well built. But the one who hears my words and does not put them into practice is like a man who built a house on the ground without a foundation. The moment the torrent struck that house, it collapsed and its destruction was complete."

Got it? Now go back and read it a couple more times, *meditating* on what Jesus is saying here. Pull it apart sentence by sentence and *listen* to His voice, His heart. Allow the Holy Spirit to speak to you.

Ponder Jesus' words on an intellectual level. What is He saying through these verses? What is a key message here? Is there a warning or a promise? Is He teaching me about God's character or my eternal destiny?

Ponder Jesus' words on a relational level. How do they apply uniquely to me? Is He calling me to action? Is He telling me to slow down and listen more? Is He encouraging me—disciplining me? Have I been neglecting Him or others?

And then get more personal:

"Here's how I feel about these verses. . ."

"Here's what's hard, God. . ."

"Help me understand, because I don't get this. . ."

"Help me move from this way of thinking to what You want. . ."

Pray through a passage: "Lord, what do You want me to do with these words?"

Through the process of Bible engagement we. . .

- *enable God's Word to shape our thinking and sharpen our ability to understand His will.* Daniel (see Daniel 7:28) and Mary (see Luke 2:19, 51) offer prime examples of why reflection on God's Word is essential to spiritual growth. Each of them faced situations in which they couldn't figure out what God was doing in their lives. Yet instead of giving up, they both did their best to carefully ponder their situations. Their actions remind us to submit to God's greater wisdom, even when His work doesn't make much sense to us.

- *saturate our minds with scripture—which can help us to battle temptation and sin.* It won't make us perfect, but it will help us to think the way God thinks. And that will help us to obey Him and to do His will. Our obedience will eventually turn into desire. Biblical meditation is actually the thoughtful contemplation of God's Word, as well as reflection on God and the person and work of Jesus Christ. It is a powerful tool when it's used with prayer and Bible reading. It doesn't have to be—as some Eastern religions teach—an emptying of our minds for the purposes of relaxation or other self-serving results. What we're talking about involves serious effort because pondering God's Word requires focus—intense mental activity coupled with emotional energy. And it's worth it.

3. Respond to God's Word

Look for ways to live out the truths of the Bible.

This is where spiritual growth really begins. Once we have received scripture and have spent ample time reflecting on it and pondering it into our lives, we must get our faith moving by *responding* to it. This is the point at which we may end up interlocking with Christ and wrestling with a hard concept or a command. But if we surrender control to God and take a step of faith, our wills begin to mesh with His.

Little by little, we grow. And step-by-step the One we're following begins a deep, sanctifying work in our souls.

Jesus says, "Give Me all of you. I'm not so concerned about your time, work, or money. I want *you*. I haven't come to torment your natural self, but to kill it. I will give you a new self instead. In fact, I will give you Myself: My own will shall become yours."

Spiritual growth and sanctification go hand in hand. And as C. S. Lewis once observed, everything that needs to be done in our souls can be done only by God:

> *Put right out of your head the idea that these are only fancy ways of saying that Christians are to read what Christ said and try to carry it out—as a man may read what Plato or Marx said and try to carry it out. They mean something much more than that. They mean that a real Person, Christ, here and now, in that very room where you are saying your prayers, is doing things to you. It is not a question of a good man who died*

*two thousand years ago. It is a living Man, still
as much a man as you, and still as much God as
He was when He created the world, really coming
and interfering with your very self; killing the old
natural self in you and replacing it with the kind
of self He has. At first, only for moments. Then for
longer periods.*

*Finally, if all goes well, turning you perma-
nently into a different sort of thing; into a new
little Christ, a being which, in its own small way,
has the same kind of life as God; which shares in
His power, joy, knowledge, and eternity.*[4]

Through the process of Bible engagement we. . .

- *have a two-way conversation with God.* As we chew on
  scripture—receiving, reflecting, and responding—and
  as we work our way through some honest questions,
  our masks come off and we begin talking to the Lord
  on a deeper, more substantive level.

- *ponder God's Word deep in our hearts.* We do this with
  a passage of scripture until the Lord's personal message has "gone right into [us] and taken possession of
  [us]"—as Dietrich Bonhoeffer said.[5] This is the level at
  which intimacy unfolds in a way that has the potential
  to change us in the deepest places of our being.

- *allow God to grow our faith in a way that's unique to each
  one of us.* Engaging the Bible this way doesn't involve
  the impersonal formulas and the rigorous, intellectual

studies that I was used to. No more cramming our heads with Bible facts, filling in the blanks of study guides, and checking off "Bible-in-a-year" reading plans. (While these traditional approaches were good at times—they certainly engage our brain—I didn't use them properly, so they didn't connect my heart in a love relationship with the one true God of the scriptures.)

Let's go back to our example from Luke 6:46–49.

After I (Mike) received this passage into my heart and mind. . .and after I had chewed on it for a while, I began feeling quite proud of himself. *I've laid my foundation on rock,* I thought. *No worries of a torrent wiping out my faith.*

But after a heart-to-heart conversation with Jesus, I began sensing a "pang" of discomfort deep in my gut. And then a guilty conscience kicked in. *Lord, are You saying that I'm not listening to You? Are there cracks in my faith? Am I doubting You?*

More reflection. More questions. And then I interlocked with Christ and wrestled with some hard truths about myself: Jesus was showing me how fear and worry were still at work in my life. And instead of trusting Him and stepping out in faith with a particular issue, I chose to maintain a controlling grip and to handle it my way. In all honesty, I wasn't hearing God's message and putting it into practice. I was heading my own way "without a foundation." And had a "torrent" struck, I would have experienced nothing short of destruction.

At first I tried to excuse my actions, and I resisted the Lord's direction. But God had my back against the wall, and I was frustrated and weary from the fight. I knew God would have His way. (Job reminds us of that, right?) I knew that the right choice was to come clean with my struggles.

Next came surrender, and then confession and repentance. After that growth.

> *We don't yet see things clearly: We're squinting in a fog, peering through a mist. But it won't be long before the weather clears and the sun shines bright. We'll see it all then, see it all as clearly as God sees us, knowing him directly just as he knows us!*
>
> *But for right now, until that completeness, we have three things to do to lead us toward that consummation: Trust steadily in God, hope unswervingly, love extravagantly. And the best of the three is love.*
>
> 1 Corinthians 13:12–13 MSG

Notes

REASON 1: CREATION AND THE CREATED MATTER

1. Charles Darwin, *The Origin of Species*, chapter 6, "Difficulties on Theory," The Talk Origins Archive, http://www.talkorigins.org/faqs/origin/chapter6.html.

2. Merriam-Webster.com, s.v. "scientific method," http://www.merriam-webster.com/dictionary/scientific%20method.

3. Encyclopaedia Britannica online, s.v. "scientific hypothesis," http://www.britannica.com/EBchecked/topic/1775842/scientific-hypothesis.

REASON 3: GOD'S WORD IS REAL. . .AND RELEVANT

1. Dr. Norman Geisler, from a lecture titled "The Bible: Uniqueness of Its Composition," delivered in Lincoln, Nebraska, May 1, 2009.

2. Eugene H. Peterson, *Eat This Book* (Grand Rapids: Eerdmans, 2006), 10–11.

3. Josh.org, "Does Archaeological Evidence Prove the Bible? How Do Archaeological Discoveries Relate to Events in Scripture?" Josh McDowell Ministry, http://www.josh.org/resources study-research/answers-to-skeptics-questions/does-archaeological-evidence-prove-the-bible/.

4. Ronald Youngblood, "Resolving 'Contradictions' in the Bible," *Moody*, September 1986, n.p.

5. David Kinnaman, *UnChristian: What a New Generation Really Thinks about Christianity* (Grand Rapids: Baker, 2007), 18.

6. Marcus J. Borg, *The Heart of Christianity* (San Francisco: HarperSanFrancisco, 2003), 6, 13.

REASON 6: RELATIONSHIPS HAVE A PURPOSE

1. Josh McDowell, *Why True Love Waits* (Carol Stream, IL: Tyndale House, 2002), 38–39.

REASON 7: LOVE AND RESPECT WIN WITH THE LGBT ISSUE

1. Joshua Harris, *Dug Down Deep* (Colorado Springs: Multnomah, 2010), 63–64.

2. Timothy J. Dailey, PhD, "Comparing the Lifestyles of Homosexual Couples to Married Couples," Family Research Council Online, http://www.frc.org/get.cfm?i=IS04C02.

REASON 8: THERE REALLY ARE OFF-BASE BELIEFS

1. Greg Stier, "My New Age Friend," CBN.com, http://www.cbn.com/spirituallife/churchandministry/evangelism/my-new_age_friend.aspx.

2. Adapted from Bill Myers and Michael Ross, *Faith Encounter* (Eugene, OR: Harvest House, 1999), 94, 128.

3. Josh.org, "Don't Genesis 1 and 2 Contain Contradictory Accounts of Creation?" Josh McDowell Ministry, http://www.josh.org/resources/study-research/answers-to-skeptics-questions/does-archaeological-

evidence-prove-the-bible/.

4. Merriam-Webster.com, s.v. "astrology," http://www.merriam-webster.com/dictionary/astrology.

REASON 9: LIFE ALWAYS MATTERS, AND IT'S VALUABLE AT EVERY AGE AND STAGE

1. James Dobson, quoted in Randy Alcorn, *Pro-Life Answers to Pro-Choice Arguments* (Colorado Springs: Multnomah, 1992), 72.

2. Randy O'Bannon, PhD, "56,662,169 Abortions in America Since Roe vs. Wade in 1973," LifeNews.com, January 12, 2014, http://www.lifenews.com/2014/01/12/56662169-abortions-in-america-since-roe-vs-wade-in-1973/.

EXTRA STUFF #1: RESOLVING "CONTRADICTIONS" IN THE BIBLE

1. Ronald Youngblood, "Resolving 'Contradictions' in the Bible," *Moody*, September 1986, n.p. Used with permission.

EXTRA STUFF #2: GET POWERED BY FOUR: A RADICAL WAY TO STUDY SCRIPTURE

1. Eugene H. Peterson, *Eat This Book* (Grand Rapids: Eerdmans, 2006), 10–11.

2. Henry T. Blackaby, *Experiencing God Day-by-Day* (Nashville: Broadman & Holman, 1998), 110.

3. Ruth Haley Barton, *Sacred Rhythms: Arranging Our Lives for Spiritual Transformation* (Downers Grove, IL: InterVarsity, 2006), 50.

4. C. S. Lewis, *Mere Christianity* (New York: Harper Collins, 1952), 164.

5. Paraphrased from Dietrich Bonhoeffer, *Life Together* (New York: Harper & Row, 1954), 83.